HID-IN-Life™ series

CUTTING

Addiction Recovery Booklets

Dr. George T. Crabb, D.O.
Steven B. Curington

TABLE OF CONTENTS

Introduction: RU Addicted 6

1. RU Tired? (Introduction to RU) 10

2. The Testimonies 20

3. The Topic 29

4. The Truth 56

5. The Transformation Through Justification 68

6. The Conformation Through Sanctification 82

7. The Reformation Through Glorification 103

INTRODUCTION
RU ADDICTED?

Addiction: medically speaking from a biblical perspective

The enormous question that faces us today is this: "Is addiction a disease?" The answer is: NO! Addiction is not a disease. But, it is a disorder. It is a disorder that can make you very sick both physically and spiritually. It is also the reason why many contract diseases. The disorder of addiction is brought on by *a* bad choice that is followed by many other bad choices.

I like to formally define addiction as "something I continue to do, even though I know it is bad for me." My friend, if you know it is bad for you, and you continue to do it, then you have a full fledged addiction. This disorder caused by addiction is a self-induced disorder of the brain. It is brought on when an individual improperly uses chemical substances and/or destructive behaviors as coping mechanisms to deal with the pain, uncertainty, disappointments, loss, and other like traumas in life.

As this behavior is repeated, physiological changes eventually occur in the brain. These changes further enhance the disorder and compel the individual to use the substance and/or destructive behavior with greater frequency and intensity. Eventually, the behavior leads to more pain, frustration, fear, uncertainty, and disappointment. The individual becomes trapped in a vicious cycle with unresolved pain as a result of engaging destructive coping mechanisms that were initially meant to alleviate the pain.

Addiction is a process that starts with a choice. That choice allows the manipulation of neurotransmitters (chemical messengers in the brain). However, through manipulation of these "feel goods," they are eventually depleted. This results in devastating destruction, depression, and ultimately death. Thus, the chasing of the "high" ends up being a futile struggle to maintain normality.

Addiction often finds its origin in a sense of personal dissatisfaction. Disappointment, anger, resentment, low self-esteem, rejection, and a host of other negative perceptions can lead an individual to search for redemption and relief in drugs, alcohol, and other self-destructive behaviors. At first, the individual discovers that the chemical or behavior not only offers relief from negative feelings, but it also offers a temporary sense of control and power.

Once the destructive behavior becomes a habit, however, the user quickly loses control and becomes the victim. Physically and emotionally dependent as well as spiritually bankrupt, the individual becomes virtually enslaved to the substance or behavior.

Because of the spiritual and emotional root causes of substance abuse and destructive behavior, along with the physical sequelae, the path to recovery must involve both spiritual, emotional, and physical correction and healing.

A life broken by substance abuse can be rebuilt, and an individual can emerge a stronger person. But, it is going to take the Truth! This book seeks to explain to you to the medical truth of your addiction, while at the same time introducing you to the spiritual Truth which will strengthen you out of your world of despair.

It is our wish that the Truth will make you free, that you may be FREED INDEED!

CHAPTER ONE
RU Tired: Cutting

RU tired? If so, try RU! At Reformers Unanimous International Addictions Program, we strive to help everyone find freedom from stubborn habits and addictions introducing them to the only Truth that makes free—Jesus Christ.

But, many other people do the same type of thing. They say, "Try Jesus!" But, after you give Him a try, they are nowhere to be found. If you are going to "give Jesus a try," you must have support to strengthen you in your trials. For to "try Jesus" as they often say, is to be "tried by Jesus."

You see, life is full of trials and turmoil. It is these trials that lead many of us to find a drug of choice to avoid the reality of life. But, there is a better way! Jesus longs to save you from this world and all its various vices. He wants to not only face your trials *with* you, He wants to face your trials *for* you!

Some think religion is a crutch. Well, if something is broken, it needs a crutch to support it while it strengthens. That is what we seek to do at RU. We seek to support you as God strengthens you over your many weaknesses in life.

I don't want you to try Jesus. Rather, I want you to just stop trying! Let God do the work in your life. He has a wonderful plan for you! My co-author and friend, Dr George Crabb, and I want to reveal that wonderful plan to you in this book.

If you are attending or would like to attend one of our hundreds of meetings that are held weekly throughout the world, we will commit to support you like a crutch. After all, that is what religion is supposed to be—God's support group. God's support system and its body of believers is found within good local churches. Every RU program in America meets in a local church or is sponsored by a local church. For this reason, we can commit to you that when you come to an RU program, you will be met by people who love God, who know God, and who are willing to serve you on behalf of God.

Below is a list of ways in which we at RU will support you as God empowers you to overcome your stubborn habits or addictions. Welcome to a ministry that has as its primary purpose love and support as you gain victory over life's vices.

THE RUI MINISTRIES STUDENT SUPPORT SYSTEM

Stories of Victory: RU tired of hearing the "war stories" of people who have no real freedom in their life? **If so, try RU!** Every week, our students share how God has changed their lives through real-life, relevant stories. This weekly forty minutes of encouraging testimonies will get your weekend started off just right.

Great Teaching: RU tired of talking about problems and doing nothing about them? **If so, try RU!** Every RU class ends with a 30-minute teaching lesson that exposes valuable Bible principles that are integral to your recovery process.

Complete Curriculum: RU tired of being told what is right and not being given the tools to determine what is right? **If so, try RU!** We have one of the best comprehensive discipleship curriculums in America. It is one of the best selling, too! Thousands of people have used our curriculum to learn the Truth about addictions and Christian apathy.

Motivational Awards: RU tired of trying to find the stamina to do the right thing in the face of mounting adversity? **If so, try RU!** We will not only encourage you and help you to do the right thing, but we will also motivate you to do so. Though an award system is just a small way of doing this, it is evidence of a program that believes in acknowledging accomplishment and rewarding participation.

Free Personal Counseling: RU tired of having to get advice from people who know little about your struggles? RU tired of having to pay hourly fees to hear yourself talk? **If so, try RU!** We offer free group and individual spiritual counseling on a wide variety of topics from addiction, to marriage, finances, family, and many other areas. You will have a leader, a helper, a director, and even the pastor available as your own personal counselors during times of urgent need.

Well-Trained Local Leadership Staff: RU tired of attending programs where the leaders and volunteer workers have the same problems as you? **If so, try RU!** Our leaders have been made free from the power of sin and can openly speak about it. They do not seek anonymity. They earnestly proclaim that Jesus is the reason for their freedom, and they have been well trained to use our program and its tools to get that salvation message to you and to those whom you love.

Exciting Children's Program: RU tired of trying to find someone to help you with your child's issues while you are still trying to deal with your many issues in life? **If so, try RU!** We will not only care for your children while you attend your class, but we will entertain, teach, and develop your children. We want them to avoid the same pitfalls that ensnared many of us. They will enjoy games, prizes, snacks, play time, awards, great teaching, and many other things. Our "Kidz Club" is the weekly highlight of every child that attends.

Clean, Well-Staffed Nurseries: RU tired of programs that will not care for your little ones? **If so, try RU!** Those programs say "come as you are." But, you "are" a family; you should be able to come "as a family." If churches can offer free nurseries, then why can't an addiction program? Our clean nurseries are well staffed by volunteers of the hosting church. These volunteers have been screened and trained; and they will love your children because they love children!

Free Transportation: RU tired of trying to find a ride to places that are wanting to and waiting to help you? **If so, try RU!** We want to pick you up and will do so for almost every one of our weekly meetings, if necessary. Though some exceptions may apply, our trained drivers are here for those of you who may be without a car or license. No questions will be asked, except your address, of course!

Weekly Fellowship Time: RU tired of being alone absent of any good friends with whom you could fellowship? **If so, try RU!** RU offers its own "Happy Hour" fellowship time at the conclusion of Friday meetings. As well, our Sunday and mid-week meetings usually offer multiple opportunities to fellowship with your fellow students and leaders. Fellowship is "R" specialty; what about "U"? Then join RU! Visitors, the *RU Happy Hour* is an optional part of our Friday night class. Refreshments and food are usually served, and served well.

Residential Treatment Centers: RU tired of trying to find residential treatment that is effective and affordable? **If so, try RU!** We operate a beautiful 100-bed facility for men and a gorgeous 40-bed facility for women at our headquarters in Rockford, Illinois. This program boasts an over 90% success rate among its graduates. We are also aware of many RU type transitional homes that may be available for your use. Please visit **www.ruhomes.org** to learn more information about our homes and to download an application.

Multi-Meeting Assemblies Weekly: RU tired of not being able to find a meeting when you need one? **If so, try RU!** We offer two to three meetings every weekend and even some during the week. Plus, we offer many activities and service opportunities for our students. Please see your RU director to find the times and days of our meetings and the hosting church's service times.

Local Church Support: "I am here to tell you that **I am not tired any more.** However, if it was not for my church, I would either be dead or a dying drug addict today!" I believe, as does your hosting church's pastor, that the local church is God's support group. It is designed by God to meet the spiritual needs of all people. When the spiritual needs of people are met, then other needs fall in line and become easier to manage. As a program, we strongly encourage you to visit the church that hosts this meeting for addicted people. Something must be different about this church if they are so willing to have this program for you. Why aren't others?

In conclusion to this chapter, I want you to understand something about this book. It is a progression of truth. What that means is that we will begin to explain things to you about **SELF-HARM and SUICIDE**. We will teach you the physical effects of **SELF-HARM and SUICIDE**, explain the soulical effects (which are the effects of your actions to your mind, will, and emotions), and expose the negative spiritual effects.

When we begin to expose the spiritual effects that your wrong behavior has had and will have on your life and your eternity, the truths will begin to progress from simple to understand to quite obscure. You may not quite comprehend everything you read, at least not at first. But, stay with it and gain the information. Your confidence in the truth taught may progress over time, but it is important that we explain it all right away and right here.

The three truths that will be expressed are called **justification**, **sanctification** and **glorification**. Those are Old English words for modern day phenomenons. They are literal experiences that will take place in everyone's life who believes in Jesus. These three experiences are what we want you to understand, as God enables you to, that you may experience a lasting victory.

Most Christian books that are written for first-time church or class visitors only explain how one can get to heaven when they die. But, they often fail to explain how to enjoy the journey there! In these topical books on addiction recovery, Dr. Crabb and I will explain truths that make up what we call the "Hidden Life," which is our life hid IN the Life of Christ (or, HID-IN-Life). We will introduce you to a pilgrimage that will give you lasting victory over your SELF-HARM and SUICIDE attempts. This pilgrimage of the HID-IN-Life will bring you a peace and joy that you may have thought was not available to the inhabitants of this world.

In conclusion, be excited about this fact. The secret that has remained hidden to you that will grant you lasting sobriety is this: The life you long for is found in a Life that longs to live withIN you!

May God be with you so that you may change ... *finally*!

Steven Curington
President and Founder
Reformers Unanimous Ministries

CHAPTER TWO
Cutting: The Testimonies

John's Testimony

Hello, my name is John. I began to cut myself when I was about ten years old. At first, I did not realize what I was doing. One day I was very angry at my parents for not letting me to do something, and I began to scratch my arms until I felt the blood come out. Somehow, this made me feel really good. I guess it was a release of all the pain I had hidden deep in my life. At that time, I thought I had found a new friend, and therefore, I continued to seek out his companionship. I began by cutting my feet and ankles, and then I started cutting my thighs. It helped me cope with situations that were out of my control. It seemed to help me, at least for the moment, forget about the anger that was deep down inside of me.

One day a friend of mine asked me if I wanted to stop. I said, "No!" I told him that it was something I needed in my life. That same friend continued to compassionately compel me to stop cutting myself. My cutting got more intense over time, and, in fact, one episode landed me in the hospital. I cut myself so deep, I cut an artery. During that hospital stay, my friend, along with an individual from his church, visited me. They lovingly told me of Someone who loved me and wanted to take all of my pain upon Himself. They explained to me the love of Jesus Christ. I knew that I needed help and could not continue down this road of destruction. They invited me to a program their church had on Friday nights. Later, I found this program to be Reformers Unanimous. During those Friday night meetings, I found Jesus Christ as my personal Savior and Friend. I have only been in the RU program for several months, but it has made a world of difference in my life. When I get the urge to cut myself now, I realize that I can go to my Savior, my Friend, and He will take that pain and anger I have deep inside and give me a calmness and peace like I've never had before.

What has helped me the most is the daily personal journal. Not only am I able to find God's message for me, but I am able to express myself to Him. In so doing, I now walk in a glorious freedom I had never experienced before.

Jamie's Testimony

I am nineteen years old, and I have just finished my first year of Bible College. I do not have a crummy or dysfunctional family. My parents are wonderful Christians. They love me unconditionally, and I love them the same. As far as my family and friends are concerned, I have it all together. But, you see, five years ago when I was fourteen, my boyfriend raped me. I am not sure if that is what made me start cutting myself, but it was not until after I was raped that I started cutting. One night, several weeks after that horrific event transpired, I was home alone. I was very upset and angry over what had transpired. I picked up a knife and started slicing my arms. I felt a relief like I had never felt before. I felt that I had found a way to control the pain I was experiencing. I liked the fact that I could control my life and feelings again. But, down deep in my heart I knew that this was not a proper avenue to take. It went against everything that I had been taught about God and His love for me.

Thankfully, the school I go to is associated with a Baptist Church that has a Reformers

Unanimous Program on Friday nights. God so graciously intervened in my life as I walked into those doors at the RU meeting. There, I learned that I did not have to destroy myself any longer to gain some temporary relief. Through the second-talk counseling, I was able to unload my burden in a very vulnerable but healthy way. With the encouragement of others in my group and working through the RU curriculum, I no longer seek to hurt myself. I now only seek a deeper, abiding relationship with Jesus Christ. I have forgiven the one that committed such a horrific crime against me. I have forgiven myself, and I now walk in freedom with my Savior, Jesus Christ.

Joe's Testimony

My name is Joe, and I am in my mid-thirties. My story begins with a good upbringing in a good, Christian home. I came to know Jesus as my personal Savior when I was a young boy. I always enjoyed going to church and learning about the Bible. I had an uneventful teenage life. I graduated from high school and went to college and earned a degree in Economics. After college I had a rough time getting a job that I really liked. I ended up in a delivery job. It met my needs, and I was somewhat satisfied. However, I always felt like I was "jipped" into taking the delivery job. I was faithful to my church, and I eventually met a godly woman. We got married. Even though my wife and I both had jobs, we were having a hard time making ends meet. It always seemed that when our bills were paid, we either had no money left over or we were actually overdrawn. This stressed my life, and it also stressed our marriage. I eventually went back to night school to further my degree and land a job that would be more satisfying. This added even more stress, as the financial picture was the same and now I was gone more from the house. Our marriage was, again, having difficulties. Because I was trying to work as much as I could and go to school, I started to miss some of the church services.

Knowing that my wife and I were running into spiritual, financial, and marital problems, I started going to our church's Reformers Unanimous Program on Friday nights. I did not fully get involved. I was very hesitant and certainly not very committed. My wife had grown somewhat cold to the things of God, and she would not even entertain the thought of going to the RU program.

I finally finished my Master's Degree and became a Certified Public Accountant. I finally landed a job that I thought was going to be the answer to all of our problems. The job was quite stressful. Eight months into my job, I was let go. This was devastating! What I thought was the answer turned out to be just another part of the problem. My wife was so upset and started to talk about divorce. I felt that I was in a deep hole. So, one morning when I woke up, I felt that the hole was so deep there was no way out. Sitting there on my couch, I realized that the only way out was to commit suicide. My wife had gone shopping that morning with her mother so I was all alone. I went to the medicine cabinet and pulled two bottles of over-the-counter medications and took them all. About two minutes after I took all that medication, my friend called me. He said that God had placed me on his heart, and he was calling to see if there was anything he could do for me. I told him what I had just done. He immediately hung up, and within the next five or ten minutes, the police and paramedics were at my door. They came in and rushed me to the hospital where I received proper medical care that saved my life.

My pastor visited me that day in the hospital, and we discussed all the things that were transpiring. He told me that the answer that I was looking for was not in a job, financial stability, and not even in marital stability. He said my answer was only found in Jesus Christ. It was not like I didn't know that, but I just needed to hear it again. My pastor encouraged me to get back into the RU program. However, this time, fully committed! I have done just that. My wife is still non-committal, and I really don't know where our relationship is going. But, I do know where my relationship with Jesus Christ is going. I have a deeper, abiding relationship with Him more now than I ever had before. I can now say that regardless where anything else goes in my life, I do have peace and freedom with my Savior, Jesus Christ. I am so sorry that I attempted to take my life, but I am so thankful for the grace of God that has allowed me another opportunity to serve Him.

John, Jamie, and Joe could not take the internal pain any longer. They saw no way to escape their pain or sense of hopelessness except through continued self-harm and suicide attempts. Like John, Jamie, and Joe, many people of all ages and walks of life battle with the seemingly undefeatable problem of self-harm and suicide on a daily basis.

Does the scenario of John, Jamie, or Joe describe you or someone you love? Are you searching for answers? There are millions of people just like you or someone you know who are desperately seeking for their way out. Like John, Jamie, and Joe, many have found that way out. They were introduced to "the Way," the Lord Jesus Christ, and have joined thousands of addicts who have found freedom through this program called **Reformers Unanimous (RU)**. RU directs people to the Truth Who makes free. I speak of the Truth named the Lord Jesus Christ. Many have come to an RU meeting, facing a combination of destructive circumstances. Many have sought help on their own, like John, Jamie, and Joe, without any long-term success. Yet, these same people are transformed as they engage in the RU curriculum and participate in its extremely supportive weekly programs.

Thousands of these individuals are now productive members of society. Collectively, they are a living testimony that there is hope for you or for those whom you love.

Yes, self-harm and suicide CAN be eliminated from your life. There is hope! There is freedom! And, that is the gospel TRUTH!

CHAPTER THREE
The Topic

Each individual that does self-harm or attempts suicide knows exactly how it makes them feel. They also recognize that the feeling it generates each time is fairly consistent. However, very few of them actually know why it makes them feel this way, much less how it happens.

As with addictive drugs, self-harm, and suicide attempts, it is amazing to learn how effective they are at masking the real root problem in a person's life. When someone is a cutter, like John and Jamie, their actions manipulate neurotransmitters in the brain that create a false sense of enjoyment and calmness. This sense of enjoyment and calmness is, of course, only temporary. As well, it is not reality. However, we have a very great Creator who made our body to secrete these neurotransmitters, and He has ways of doing so without the pain and misery of trying to harm ourselves.

NEUROTRANSMITTERS AND THEIR ROLES IN THE BODY:
- acetylcholine: stimulates muscles, aids in sleep cycle

- **norepinephrine**: similar to adrenaline, increases heart rate; helps form memories
- **GABA** (gamma-aminobutyric acid): prevents anxiety
- **glutamate**: aids in memory formation
- **serotonin**: regulates mood and emotion
- **endorphin**: necessary for pleasure and pain reduction
- **dopamine**: motivation; pleasure

In this chapter, Dr. George Crabb, a board certified Internal Medicine physician and member of the American Society of Addiction Medicine, will explain to us the phenomenon and feeling behind the self-harm and suicide behavior that plagues many.

THE TOPIC: SELF-HARM

Can you imagine slicing your stomach with a razor blade or carving a design in your arm? How about burning your fingertips with a cigarette or scorching your palms with a lighter? Do you think you could ever intentionally break a finger, arm, foot, or a leg just because you wanted to? These are some of the activities behind self-harm. Most of

> **SELF-HARM FACT**
> **Types of Self-Injurious Behavior**
> Cutting, Carving, or Slicing Skin
> Burning
> Biting or Chewing
> Whipping
> Scratching
> Head Banging
> Hair Pulling
> Intentionally Bruising or Breaking Bones
> Starvation or Binging & Purging
> Excessive Body Piercing
> Excessive Tattooing

the individuals that engage in self-harm behavior never thought they could do the above activities. But, now that they've started and experienced the calmness and sense of control from this behavior, they now find it hard to stop. In fact, they have become addicted to this self-harm behavior.

The testimonies of John and Jamie reflect some of the paradoxes of self-injury. They hate and like what they do. They want and don't want to stop. They cut, burn, and bruise themselves, but they do not want to kill themselves. They find shame and comfort in their scars.

Self-harm or self-injury is also known as "self-injurious behavior" (SIB). This includes such activity as self-mutilazation, cutting, self-abuse, and parasuicidal behavior. For all practical purposes, self-harm is a widely-misunderstood phenomenon, characterized by repeated, deliberate, non-lethal harming of one's body. The greatest misunderstanding about self-harm is the assumption that self-injurers, like John and Jamie, want to die, and that their self-injurious behaviors are just failed attempts at suicide. This is not necessarily the case. I have found the best way to describe the reasons for self-injury, and they are as follows:

1. Self-injurers commonly report that they fill empty inside.
2. Self-injurers commonly report that they are under or over stimulated.
3. Self-injurers commonly report that they are unable to express their feelings.
4. Self-injurers commonly report that they are not understood by others.
5. Self-injurers commonly report that they are fearful to intimate relationships.

Self-injury is their way to cope with or relieve

painful or hard to express feelings, and it is generally not a suicide attempt. In other words, self-injurers harm themselves in order to help themselves.

It is estimated that nearly one percent of the United States' population are self-injurers. Most are females like Jamie. As with John and Jamie, most self-injurers start harming themselves in their pre-teen or teenage years. Over fifty percent of self-injurers, like Jamie, were sexually abused. Many self-injurers deal with depression and severe anxiety disorders. Those that self-harm come in all shapes, sizes, and colors. Outward issues do not determine whether or not someone becomes a self-injurer. It has more to do with an inward inability to express feelings or cope with strong emotions.

The primary reason people self-injure is to relieve emotional pain. It is an extreme, unhealthy, and ungodly coping mechanism that some people use to get through times of stress, anxiety, conflict, disappointment, failure, or heartache. Many self-injurers have never developed the ability to feel or express emotions in a healthy way. Self-injury provides relief, albeit temporary, from the pressure of pinned-up feelings. One individual in my office who was a self-injurer said to me, "I felt my emotional pain drain away with my blood. It is as though punching a hole in my skin deflated this balloon of intense, overwhelming feelings. The air of pain came out slowly, and the release only lasted a short time, but it gave me a much-needed release." This sense of release and euphoria comes from the same mechanism that cocaine and other drugs produce in the body. This is a temporary surge of the neurotransmitters in the brain. I have had other self-injurers tell me that they harm themselves in order to feel something or feel anything at all. They are numb emotionally. They have gone on to tell me that physical pain helps them acknowledge their emotional pain. Another described it this way: "It's like I was dead inside, and by cutting myself, it reminded me that I was still alive and could still feel something." Some self-injurers like Jamie, because of past events, are punishing themselves or expressing self-hatred. They don't want to die; they just want to blame, criticize, or punish themselves. This is not only

> **SELF-HARM FACT**
> **Hidden Dangers of Self-Harm**
> Addiction
> Infection
> Permanent Scaring
> Escalating Injuries
> Long-Term Health Effects
> Unintentional Suicide

true for those who have been abused sexually but also physically and emotionally. They replay imaginary video tapes of messages they heard from their abusers in their minds over and over again. Some of these statements they hear in their minds are:

- You are worthless.
- It is your fault.
- You deserve to be punished.
- You are bad.
- You have to pay.

In self-injurers' minds, cutting themselves serve two purposes: (1) It punishes them with pain, and (2) It allows some of their badness to seep out with their blood. It is a way for them to make up for their badness.

Self-injury can bring out a host of emotions, especially from people who do not understand the condition. These emotions can include:

- **Shock**
- **Revulsion**
- **Anger**
- **Fear**
- **Disgust**
- **Shame**
- **Condemnation**

Self-injurers have already felt these things about themselves, especially shame. Shame is what makes self-injurers wear long sleeves all summer long. They cover their scars and hide their injuries so nobody will know what they are doing. Shame is an incredibly strong, self-condemning emotion that keeps individuals, like John and Jamie, feeling badly about themselves and trapped in a cycle of self-destruction.

Self-injury is just as addictive as drugs,

> **SELF-HARM FACT**
> While many do, some self-injurers do not feel any pain when they cut or burn themselves. The predominant feeling is relief.

pornography, or tobacco. Remember, no one can make self-injurers stop hurting themselves. This is a choice that they can only make for themselves. However, it is a choice that they may need support to reach.

Another type of self-injury is eating disorders. These attempts at self-harm, whether starvation (Anorexia Nervosa), binging and purging (Bulimia), or extreme over-eating (Binge Eating Disorder), are covered in a separate subject book entitled, <u>Eating</u>.

I am often asked by a loved one, "How can I tell if my friend or loved one is self-injuring themselves?" The following are guidelines to help you evaluate the situation:

1. Does your friend or loved one have cuts or scars on their arms or legs?
2. Does your friend or loved one try to keep you from seeing their scars?
3. Does your friend or loved one wear long pants and long-sleeve shirts in hot weather?

4. Does your friend or loved one offer lame explanations for their injuries, i.e., "The cat scratched me."
5. Does your friend or loved one show signs of depression or anger?

If your friend or loved one answered **YES** <u>to any of the above questions</u>, it could indicate that they are engaging in self-harm behavior. Again, the above is not an exhaustive list, but it is information to help you evaluate the situation your friend or loved one may be in.

In closing this section on self-harm, just remember that all self-injury behaviors are silent cries for help.

THE TOPIC: SUICIDE

What is most troubling is that the suicide rate for people nineteen and under has increased in recent years. Adults may find these statistics shocking, but most young people are well aware of the problem.

Another troubling revelation in the Gallop Youth Survey's poll was the number of respondents who admitted that they have entertained notions of committing suicide. Some twenty-five percent

> **SUICIDE FACT**
> According to the Gallop Youth Survey, many teens feel alienated from society and admit to feeling confused, pressured, afraid, and angry.

of the respondents answered YES to this question, with seven percent admitting that they had at least taken initial steps to actually committing the act. It is estimated that one in 12,500 people between the ages of fifteen and nineteen can be expected to commit suicide. For children between the ages of ten and fourteen, the suicide rate is one in 100,000. This number may seem small, but it represents a huge problem. Boys are more likely to commit suicide than girls. It is my opinion that suicide is an emotional cancer of the soul. It truly is a silent crisis as Joe demonstrated in his life. This is a major dilemma for our churches, schools, and our nation. For the most part, the issue of suicide has remained unaddressed or inadequately responded to.

People find many reasons to take their own lives. Amongst the more frequent reasons why people attempt suicide are substance-abuse

> **SUICIDE FACT**
> The rate of suicide among older people is even greater than the rate among young adults.

problems. Individuals having a difficult time coping with trouble at home, school, work, or finances (as was Joe's case), contemplate suicide much more than those who don't. Victims always show many warning signs.

Teenagers often have difficulty coping with life's challenges. In 1997, the Gallop Youth Survey published a "Teen Alienation Index." In that survey, twenty percent of the teenagers admitted to feeling confused, pressured, ignored, bored, afraid, angry, or tired. These teenagers also admitted to harboring thoughts of doing violence to themselves or others. Suicide is, of course, a problem that affects more than just teenagers. For people between the ages of twenty-five and thirty-four, suicide is the second-highest cause of death. For people between the ages of thirty-five and forty-four, it is the fourth highest cause of death. Overall, suicide is the eleventh highest cause of death in the United States.

It is estimated that every seventeen minutes, an American takes his or her own life. When a person does commit suicide, it devastates family, friends, and even their community. Just as awful is what may happen if the suicide attempt fails. Some people recover from their attempts to kill themselves, as was the case of Joe we read about earlier. But, what happens to the person who attempts suicide and fails and is forced to live with the wounds for the rest of his or her life? The damage caused by a failed suicide attempt may be physical as well as emotional. These individuals can be disabled with brain damage, confined to a wheelchair, or unable to work or enjoy a full life. According to the National Institute of Mental Health, as many as twenty-five unsuccessful suicide attempts are made for every attempt that is successful.

After the suicide attempt, one must face the reality of having made such a ghastly choice! This can be a daunting task. The suicide attempt of an individual can do more than traumatize the victim's family and friends. Sometimes, a whole community can feel the pain. There is a

> **SUICIDE FACT**
> For some teenagers, the stress caused by family problems may become too much to handle.

phenomenon called *suicide contagion*. According to the National Institute of Mental Health, one suicide can sometimes lead to another. In other words, the suicides could become contagious. Typically, suicide contagion occurs when the victim is exposed to a suicide committed by a friend or family member or through media reports of suicide.

One of the warning signs of someone potentially contemplating suicide, and a warning sign that Joe had in his life, was mood swings. Mood changes may not necessarily be toward sadness, though. People who were formerly quiet may become hyperactive. People who were friendly and outgoing may become withdrawn. Some people will become depressed, have trouble getting out of bed, not sleeping well at night, napping throughout the day, or waking up early in the morning and unable to return to sleep. Others may have changes in their appetites.

They will begin to lose or gain weight rapidly. They may start to feel restless or uncomfortable around family and friends. Joe found it difficult to concentrate, and he started losing interest in hobbies and other activities that he once enjoyed. Others may start giving away their possessions preparing for their death. Older people, who prepare for suicide, may make out a will or make revisions to a will that already exists. Potential suicide victims may make a half-hearted attempt to kill themselves using a method they think will not work. Or, they may start taking risks with their lives, like driving recklessly. They may even start drinking alcohol and taking drugs. They can also lose interest in their personal appearance, and as in Joe's case, become preoccupied with death. Joe found himself entertaining thoughts that life was not worth living.

Research indicates that young people are often quite verbal with their intentions when they are contemplating suicide. They may make the following statements:

1. I would be better off dead!
2. Nothing matters, it is no use.

Who is at risk for suicide? Suicide among young people is a problem that is growing at an alarming rate. However, it is the elderly, particularly older, white males, who are most likely to commit suicide. Among white males sixty-five and older, risk goes up with age. Males eighty-five and older have a suicide rate that is six times that of the overall national rate. However, statistics indicate that anyone can fall prey to suicide. In fact, any young person can fall victim to suicide, i.e., straight-A students, athletes, gifted students, and the like. Students who struggle in school or students who simply seem to blend into the crowd are also at risk. But, there are many things that are common among suicide victims as illustrated in Joe's life. They experience strong feelings of stress, confusion, self-doubt, pressure to succeed, financial uncertainty, and other fears of the future. For teenagers, some may find the breakup of their parents' marriage too traumatic

SUICIDE FACT
The abuse of alcohol or drugs can lead to suicidal behavior.

to face. Others may harbor deep feelings of stress over the remarriage of their parents and the formation of new families, in which they are forced to share a home with step parents or new siblings. Maybe the divorce forced them to move to a new community and enroll in a new school where they have no friends. Suicide offers a solution to these seemingly, insurmountable problems. One trend is the rise in suicide rates on college campuses. According to statistics compiled by the National Mental Health Association, suicide is the second-leading cause of death among people of college age. Some of the reasons for this trend among college students are obvious:

- College students find themselves away from home for the first time.

- College students are confronted with an unfamiliar environment.

- College students don't have their family and friends to rely on if they need help.

- College students generally find it hard to cope at college for the first time.

Another well-known fact is the relationship between alcohol and drug use in suicidal behavior. A review of suicides among young people between the ages of eighteen and twenty found that drinking alcohol was associated with higher youth suicide rates. In studies that examine risk factors among people that have completed suicide, drug and alcohol abuse occurs more frequently among young people compared to older persons. Alcohol and drug abuse lead many people down a road of hopelessness and despair. People consider suicide when they are hopeless and unable to see alternative solutions to their problems. Most suicide victims believe they have become a burden on others.

There is another strong association and that is suicide and eating disorders. Recent studies have demonstrated a link to suicide with eating disorders, specifically Bulimia Nervosa. Bulimia Nervosa is an eating disorder that primarily affects adolescent girls and young women. Individuals who suffer from Bulimia Nervosa stuff themselves with food (this is called binge eating or binging), then they force themselves to vomit or use laxatives (this is known as purging) to get rid of the food they just ate. Girls who suffer from Bulimia Nervosa have a morbid fear of getting fat. It is similar to the eating disorder known as Anorexia Nervosa in which girls starve themselves. In 1998, a poll taken by the Gallop Youth Survey found that ninety-two percent of the five-hundred teenagers questioned worry about what they weigh. There are many similarities among people who exhibit symptoms of Bulimia Nervosa and people who talk about suicide or try to kill themselves. Bulimia Nervosa is an addictive behavior much like drug or alcohol abuse. I have had many bulimics tell me that they find the cycles of binge eating and purging to be a way in which they relieve anxiety, which is the same way individuals seek release from cares through drugs.

Many people who have survived their suicide attempts have reported feeling better about themselves as though the attempt to do physical harm helped them find a release from their tensions and anxieties.

Another issue that must be addressed in regards to suicide is the violence in the entertainment media. The first suicide depicted in a theatre was probably in 1595 when William Shakespeare's play, *Romeo and Juliet*, made its debut. The often-told and often-mimicked story is now quite familiar. Two teenagers defy their families by falling in love. When events and enemies conspire against them, their story ends in tragedy – they take their own lives! The progression of violence from that time until now has intensified greatly. During the past forty years, there have been more than one thousand studies on the effects of media violence. Most of them have drawn similar conclusions: VIOLENCE IN THE ENTERTAINMENT MEDIA LEADS TO REAL-WORLD VIOLENCE. In 1999, a report to the U.S. Senate Judiciary Committee contained these statistics:

1. **The average teenager listens to 10,500 hours or rock music between the seventh and twelfth grades.**

2. **In a typical 18-hour day of television programming, a viewer can observe an average of five violent acts per hour.**

3. One study of media violence focused on the programming available on ten channels and found 1,846 acts of violence depicted in a single day.

4. By age 18, the typical teenager will have seen 200,000 acts of violence on television, including 16,000 simulated murders.

The report did not just focus on television, but it cited the increasing reliance on violence in movies, music, and video games.

The 1999 Senate Judiciary Committee Report commented: *A preference for heavy metal music may be a significant marker for alienation, substance abuse, psychiatric disorders, suicide risk, sex-role stereotyping, and risk-taking behaviors during adolescence.*

The result of inundating young people with violent entertainment is quite obvious. They have become desensitized to violence, meaning they don't appreciate violent content for what it truly is.

SUICIDE FACT
Most suicide victims believe they have become a burden on others.

The Senate Judiciary Committee Report went on to report: *Having fed our children death and horror as entertainment, we should not be surprised by the outcome.* In 1977 when the Gallop Organization first asked teenagers between the ages of thirteen and seventeen whether they felt there was too much violence in the movies, forty-two percent agreed. A total of 502 American teenagers participated in that poll. In 1999, twenty-two years later, the Gallop Organization asked the same question of 502 teenagers. This time, twenty-three percent of the respondents said they thought movies were too violent. What happened during the twenty-two years in between? It's only obvious! Teenagers were inundated with thousands and thousands of hours of violence in the movies, television, music, and video games. Someone who grows up in a world where violence is common, they may not find stabbings, shootings, or poisonings in movies all that violent. Violence is to the entertainment world what nicotine is to cigarettes. The reason why the media has to pump more violence into us is because we have built up a tolerance. In order to get the same "high," we need ever-higher levels of violence. The television industry has gained its market share through an addictive and toxic ingredient.

NOTE: There is no question, though, that the one factor that attributes to most young adult suicides is drug abuse.

Approximately seven years ago, I was called down to the emergency room to help revive a seventeen year old who attempted suicide by hanging. The whole medical team worked feverously for more than thirty minutes in an attempt to revive this young man. Sorry to say, we were unsuccessful. Toxicology reports found massive amounts of alcohol and opiates in his system. After this young man was pronounced dead, the medical personnel found this fragmented note in his jeans. It stated, "I just want to scream and cry. I can't understand why I feel this way, as if my life were cursed at birth. But, I know that I have failed at life, and it is so much easier to just drop out. Please try and understand that this is for the best. Life was just unbearable. Please forgive me mom and dad." The note was signed, "I love you, Mark."

It is estimated that in the United States, some eleven million teenagers under the age of eighteen have tasted alcohol and many drink regularly. Drugs are another matter. Despite the ongoing war on drugs such as marijuana, cocaine, heroin, and LSD, drugs still remain readily available in and around schools throughout the United States. Illegal drugs are only a part of the problem. Many teenagers have access to prescription medications in the possession of older family members or friends. Medications such as tranquilizers, pain killers, and sedatives often produce some degree of narcotic effect. Even non-prescription medications cannot be ruled out. One study found that sixty-four percent of young people who tried to take their own lives by overdose made the attempt by using over-the-counter medications, which are available in any pharmacy in America to anyone with the money to buy them. Studies have concluded that there is a definite link between substance abuse and suicide. A 1989 report on teenage suicide prepared by the U.S. Alcohol, Drug Abuse & Mental Health Administration stated, "Analysis of data for adolescents…

document a close association between substance abuse and suicide." Young people who abuse drugs and alcohol were up to eight times more likely to kill themselves than teenagers who don't drink or take drugs.

You see, in many cases, depressed, stressed, or despondent young people turn to drugs and alcohol as a way of drowning their troubles. They hope that by taking a drink or getting high, they will find relief from their anxieties. Of course, this solution does not work! Once the drug or the drink wears off, all their troubles return. Meanwhile, the adolescent has added a new problem to his woes – ABUSE OF ALCOHOL AND DRUGS! Alcohol and drugs, without exception, make a bad problem worse.

As we know, suicide is an impulsive act, so drugs and alcohol will make a teenager act impulsively, thus, commit suicide. Some drugs are hallucinogens. LSD (known as acid) and PCP (angel dust) may cause their users to hallucinate and totally lose touch with reality while they are under the influence. In some cases, users of hallucinogenic drugs experience violent or suicidal feelings. Sometimes, young people start thinking about suicide because of their alcohol and drug problems. When they started using drugs and drinking alcohol, they were not suicidal or in any way depressed. They may have just been experimenting with the alcohol and drugs. Soon, they become alcoholics and drug addicts. Their lives cave in around them. They become alienated from their family and friends. They sink into deep fits of despair as they find themselves unable to shake their habits and straighten out their lives. In the meantime, their alcohol and drug addiction grows worse. Finally, feeling no way out, they turn to suicide.

There is no question that a stable home life can be a deterrent to suicide. Sadly, stability is often lacking in many American homes. Young people who learn they are capable of accomplishing great things through the power or God generally do not look for reasons to kill themselves. Getting young people involved in church and school are also deterrents to teen suicide. Many potential suicide victims feel alienated. They are loners who think no one cares about them. Oh, but Somebody does care about them! So, no matter where you may be in your contemplation of life, I want to share with you that there is hope. There is Someone that cares, and that someone is Jesus Christ!

All that John, Jamie, Joe, and the other millions of individuals in our society today are looking for is help to heal the hurt that lives down deep within them.

Friend, regardless of where you may be in your struggle with self-harm or attempted suicide, the good news is that there is life after self-harm and suicide. John, Jamie, and Joe found this life. For this to be accomplished in your life, there must be a change in your behavior. I want you to know that the only effective way of changing your behavior is changing the beliefs to which you hold. This will be the subject of the remainder of this book.

CHAPTER FOUR
The Truth

When viewing the world of self-harm or suicide, one often envisions a scenario of total victimization. But, the cold reality of self-harm and suicide is that it is a deliberate, destructive *choice* made by the user that is followed by many similar bad choices. In other words, it is a lifestyle of repetitive, bad choices. Bad choices will be made in nearly every area of a user's life because of this single bad choice to commit self-harm or suicide, even once!

Self-harm or suicide is a release for the user, albeit, temporary. It relieves the pain that dwells in the deepest, darkest dungeon of one's life. A user may be thinking, "It is no big deal!" Choosing to believe that is merely one's attempt to minimize and deflect attention away from their problem. My friend, alcoholism is a big deal. It is a major issue that affects the body, soul, and spirit of an individual. You may think it is a necessary ingredient for having a good time and getting your work done, but oh how far from the truth is that lie?!

However, if you picked up this book at an RU class or received it in some way from someone who cares about you, then you might by thinking, "I know someone like that!" Or, you may even say, "That's me!"

So, why do you do what you do? The reasons behind your destructive behavior are many. Perhaps the most common reason for committing self-harm or suicide is because it is a coping mechanism.

All of us learn to handle stressful and negative events in different ways. We feel "out of control" because of internal pain, frustration, and anxiety. Our natural response is to alleviate the pain. Unfortunately, many people find temporary relief in doing harm to themselves.

Dr. Crabb is 100 percent correct. If you find yourself living your life this way, then you have developed an unhealthy coping mechanism. A coping mechanism is simply how a person chooses to deal with disappointments. Prior to my role as Reformers Unanimous President and Founder, I was addicted to powder cocaine and alcohol for over ten years. Whenever I would use cocaine or alcohol, the overwhelming difficulties from which I was running seemed to disappear.

I believe that our many inner hurts is what creates our desire to escape reality. That internal hurt drives one to use drugs, drink alcohol, do self-harm, or commit suicide as a way to relieve the pain. But, unfortunately, the pain and hurt is always still there.

As someone who personally knows the bondage of cocaine and alcohol and has found freedom from their gripping control, I want you to know that believing your hard or hurt feelings are best handled with the coping mechanisms of methamphetamine, cocaine, alcohol, another mood altering drug, self-harm, or suicide is an absolute lie. It is a lie from your spiritual enemy, Satan, who seeks to entrap then destroy you. Our desire is to reveal to you the Truth. If you will choose to reject any lies you have believed and choose to live in this Truth you are learning, then the power the lies possess over you will be broken. The Bible promises those who Jesus has made free are freed indeed (see John 8:36 at the back of this book for actual Bible wording)!

Self-harm or suicide is only a temporary fix. It does not remove the pain caused by your unmet needs. It simply temporarily masks it. The condemnation and feelings of guilt and shame that many addicts carry from past failures, abuses, or unhealthy relationships inside and outside the family can lead to a self-hatred deep in their soul for which they desperately desire relief.

You have turned to self-harm or suicide, choosing it to be your preferred way of dealing with this internal turmoil. This improperly handled internal turmoil eventually leads the user to become depressed. Depression then facilitates the use of more self-harm or an excuse to commit suicide. Always remember this: Depression **can** and usually **will** control your entire life.

Feelings of depression lead a person to feel that they have no control and that things will never change. They feel they are in a deep, dark hole with no legitimate way out. They see the only way out to escape their mental anguish is to do self-harm or commit suicide. Depression coupled with alcohol and drug abuse can be a life-threatening combination, as it can be a major factor in causing an individual to do self-harm or commit suicide.

A self-harm or suicide individual's thinking is all based on a lie. Having accepted this lie, they now have a distorted view of reality. Their whole concept of life has become skewed. How could someone come to believe that something so damaging and destructive, like self-harm or suicide, can bring relief? The answer is found in this truth: Wrong behavior is *stimulated* by a process of wrong thinking. Wrong thinking is *permeated* by wrong beliefs.

To change our behavior, we must change our thinking. And, to change our thinking, we will need to change a great many of our wrong beliefs about ourselves, God, and even about others. In other words, our beliefs must be dealt with in order to experience eventual, true and lasting freedom.

So, we see that self-harm or contemplated suicide is a vicious cycle with no apparent way out. However, there is a way of escape! I have escaped and am no longer an addict. John, Jamie, and Joe have escaped and gone on to live successful lives, as have I. You have tried to find your own way of escape, haven't you? It has not happened. You have constantly failed. Your failures have only increased your desire to do self-harm or contemplate suicide, and its hold on your life just leads to deeper pain. But, the Bible has the answer.

Jesus, whom in John 8:32 tells us is "the Truth," beckons for you to turn to Him. He wants to break the chains that hold you in bondage. He wants to restore and comfort you into a right relationship to God, to others, and even to ourselves.

Dr. Crabb is an expert on addiction recovery. As a member of the American Society of Addiction Medicine, he has partnered with me and our ministry to help everyone understand that the real bondage of addiction is not physical, or even mental. It is spiritual.

> "THE CRITICAL NEEDS OF OUR BODY AND SOUL – SIGNIFICANCE, SECURITY, PURPOSE, AND IDENTITY – CAN ONLY BE MET THROUGH HIS SPIRIT EMPOWERING US." –DR. GEORGE CRABB

The Truth of Jesus and the truths of Jesus will give you a life of joy. Jesus called it an "abundant life." But, how do you find Him? And, how do you find the submission to Him necessary to be made free?

Those are good questions. Allow me to introduce to you the Answer, Jesus Christ. He is the answer that John, Jamie, Joe, and I have found in our quest to be cured of our cocaine, alcohol, self-harm, and suicidal addictions. Jesus is the only One who can touch your heart so deeply that your life can literally change forever.

Our media tends to portray Christians in a very unattractive way. They even like to make them look stupid or "extra dependant" on a crutch of some sort to get through life. I've heard it said on national television by a well known actor that "Christians are weak people who can't stand the thought that they only have one life, so live it up! They just gotta' believe in giving this life up for some hope of another world that doesn't exist!"

Can I ask a question? How would a Hollywood actor know if there is another world? And, if he is wrong and I am right, how sorry would he be that he was on the wrong end of that opinion.

It is sad that Christians are portrayed on television and in movies as idiots because this portrayal has a profound impact on those who are so gullible to society's ways of manipulation. The truth is that very smart people, many presidents, kings, mega large corporate CEO's, and millions of others profess themselves to be believers in Jesus Christ as their only way to Heaven. Are they stupid, gullible, or in need of some crutch? I would say not.

As a matter of fact, you know what? They are happy people! A great many of them live victorious lives over vice. It is almost unheard of for a Christian to commit suicide. There must be a reason why so many rich or famous people who do not possess Christ profess such misery in life. They are unable to find any satisfaction though they have tried and tried and tried.

Yes, the world is influenced by Hollywood actors, media moguls and personalities, millions of other CEO's who are miserable; but there are even more engineers, machinists, construction workers, secretaries, wait-staff, and busy mothers who do not know this Christ of whom I speak. Glaringly, you can see their lifestyle bound to selfish pride, ingratitude, depression, and many other debilitating behaviors.

I think it is easier to believe in a Creator that put you here for a reason and wants you to be at peace with Him and to fulfill that reason for your existence than it is to believe, "We only live once—enjoy it!" Boy, I would hate to be wrong on that decision and live eternity in hell because I would rather continue in wrong and never be forgiven for it.

Jesus came to make us free. He will make you free from guilt, shame, condemnation, and hatred. He will make you free to enjoy a life of peace, joy, satisfaction, and among other things, sobriety. Jesus will illuminate the root causes of your addiction. Not only will He show you the problem, He will show you the answer to your problem. Jesus will never harm, hurt, or betray you. The love Jesus has for you will never change because His love is not based on you or your performance, but solely based on His character, which never, ever changes.

The Bible tells us that, to conform our lives to something worthwhile and fulfilling, we must transform the way that we think. (See Romans 12:2 in the back of this book.) Transformation is the word *metamorphosis*. It means "to change in form." In this case, we want to change our forms of thinking. The best way to change our way of thinking is not to "try" to think differently, but rather to first change the way we believe. When our beliefs change, then so can our thoughts.

For example, you remember the super hero the Incredible Hulk? Whenever his alter ego, David Bruce Banner, became angry or outraged, a startling "metamorphosis" occurred. He went from being calm, cool, and collected to a raging monster because he struggled to handle adversity. Anger was a trigger that changed this otherwise calmed man into the form of a monster. That was a negative and dangerous transformation.

However, there was another super hero that was far more "mild mannered." I am speaking of Clark Kent. Clark Kent never broke a sweat when faced with adversity. How could he stay so calm, so cool, and so collected no matter the level of threat he faced? It was because he knew he had a power living within him that gave him supernatural abilities. Clark Kent, remembering this during extremely difficult times, made it possible for himself to "transform" into a dependable person in times of trouble.

Well, that is the transformation we all need! And, that, my friend, is the transformation that RU wants you to experience. Not a transformation in which you become a super hero, but one in whom you become Supernatural.

There are three benefits of salvation (accepting the truth…JESUS): justification, sanctification, and glorification. It is these benefits that grant us not only the freedom from sin's *penalty*, but also the freedom from sin's *power*, and eventual freedom from sins' *presence*.

In our next chapter, we will explain to you how to have your payment for your sin debt (death and hell) paid by the One who died for all. We want everyone who attends our classes to clearly understand how they can accept Jesus Christ, the Truth, as their personal Savior. We will do this here for you by explaining to you God's Simple Plan of Justification. It comes from a complete transformation.

CHAPTER FIVE
Our Transformation Through Justification

Now, I understand that the purchase of this book indicates that you or someone you love struggles with self-harm or suicidal tendencies. And you probably were not necessarily interested in finding religion; you want to find FREEDOM! But, my friend, there is no freedom without the Son of God. If you want to be freed, you will have to go through the only Way that grants freedom. You gain freedom through the sacrifices made on our behalf by Jesus Christ.

Jesus wants to help you! He has already provided a way of escape for you. Choosing to continue in your attempt to do self-harm or contemplate suicide is, in essence, denying and rejecting the freedom Jesus offers to you. Trying to construct your own answers to your addiction or even your other problems in life is like saying that the torture Jesus went through for you on the cross was not enough. He would need to do more for you to turn to Him.

No! His death was enough to pay not only the

penalty for your sin, but also to provide you with the emancipation from the power of your sin, as well. Yes, true freedom begins by accepting Jesus Christ's substitutionary death on the cross as your penalty payment for all the wrong you have ever committed. All of it, one payment. God's sinless Son died for you. We refer to this as "accepting Christ as your Savior."

If you have never done this in your life, there is no other step, much less twelve steps you can take to find freedom. This is a "change in belief" that each individual must make for themselves. It is the most important choice you will ever make.

Justification is a benefit that takes place at the moment of salvation. Justification is salvation from the *penalty* of sin (which is the Bible word for our wrongs). The penalty from which we are being justified is the penalty of eternal separation from God in a place called Hell.

To help you picture what Christ has done for you and me, there are some key words in the Bible I want to help you understand. What Jesus Christ actually did **for us** needs to be understood before we can clearly accept His gift and establish the pathway to freedom from our addictive nature.

SIN

Sin is the Bible word for our wrong. The Bible tells us that everyone does things wrong and everyone does wrong things. This makes us sinners. (See Romans 3:23)

Our wrongs must be paid for in some way and someday. It is a huge debt! The Bible tells us the payment for our wrong doing is death. (See Romans 6:23)

We are all sinners and so are you. Your drug of choice is just one of the many sin problems that you have. You may think the best choice you could make is to avoid doing self-harm to yourself or attempting suicide. But, the worst choice you can make is to die as an unconverted sinner. You will spend eternity in hell.

Do you really believe that you are a sinner? As you enter our program, ask yourself this question. "Do I realize I am a sinner, and that my sin deems me worthy of hell?" If you do not know this, your beliefs must change, my friend, if you are going to be made free in life.

Step One: Accept the fact that you are a sinner. Express to God in dependence upon Him your agreement with the Bible that you are indeed a wrong doer, a sinner!

DEATH

Death means to be absent of life. The Bible tells us that because of sin, God determined that man would become mortal. As a result of that decision, eventually each person physically dies because of our wrong doing. (See Romans 5:12)

However, if we die in our sins, we are destined for hell and separated from God for eternity. Hell is God's judgment and final rejection of the lost. But, it is not a rejection because of our imperfection; it is judgment for our rejection! God loves us, even as sinners, but our sin exempts us from our ability to enjoy Heaven (for those who do not accept His free gift of Salvation).

That free gift was borne by God's Son, Jesus, who willingly offered His own life as a substitute to pay for our debt. Jesus paid our sin debt when He willingly submitted to die for us by being crucified on the cross. (See Romans 5:8)

Do you believe that Jesus died for you and me? If not, please remember that our beliefs must change, my friend, if we are going to be made free in life. Please don't die refusing to believe that you are a sinner and that Jesus died for you.

Step Two: As you continue your prayer from step one, agree with the Bible through your own personal dependence that Jesus died for your sins.

BURIAL

The Bible tells us that after Jesus died, His followers borrowed the tomb of a wealthy believer and laid Jesus' body to rest in that tomb. It was guarded every hour of the day by Roman soldiers. (See Matthew 27:62-65) After three whole days, some close friends of Jesus came to visit the tomb, and found it empty! The body of Jesus was missing! Some thought He had been stolen. But, the Bible says that an angel of the Lord was sitting nearby and informed Jesus' friends that He was gone, for He had risen from the dead. (See Matthew 28:5-7)

Do you believe that Jesus was buried for you? If not, please remember that our beliefs must change, my friend, if we are going to be made free in life. Please don't die refusing to believe that you are a sinner and that Jesus died and was buried for you.

Step Three: As you continue your prayer from step two, agree with the Bible through your own personal dependence that Jesus was buried and laid in state for three whole days.

RESURRECTION

Resurrection means "brought back to life." The Bible tells us that God the Father raised Jesus, His Son, from the dead through the power of His Holy Spirit. (See First Peter 3:18.) Yes, after being crucified and lying in a tomb for three days, Jesus came out of the grave alive! Hundreds of eye witnesses saw Him, proving that this phenomenon is truth.

You see, God is love. God loved us so much

that He sent His Son to die for us (See John 3:16.), and He loved His Son so much that He raised Him from the dead. You see, death's power over us would not have been conquered unless God could demonstrate His power over it. Thus, the resurrection of Jesus is important to understanding what He has done for us. Yes, God has power over life, and He has power over death. He can give us the *promise* of His life, and He can save us from our *penalty* of our death.

Do you believe that Jesus was resurrected from the dead by God through the power of His Holy Spirit? If not, please remember that our beliefs must change, my friend, if we are going to be made free in life. Please don't die refusing to believe that you are a sinner, that Jesus died, was buried, and rose from the dead the third day.

Step Four: As you continue your prayer from step three, agree with the Bible through your own personal dependence that you believe that Jesus rose from the dead after three days, by the empowering Holy Spirit.

These three simple words—death, burial, and resurrection—are three words that represent the miracle events that provide us freedom from the penalty of our sins. Receiving this payment frees us from paying the debt for our sin. If you have accepted this gift, then according to the Bible, you now have a home in heaven reserved for you. We do not get to heaven based on what we have done, but by believing in what Christ has done *for* us. We have to believe by dependence on the events described in these three words in order to be saved from Hell and granted a home in Heaven.

That brings us to our final two important word definitions. Those final two words are "believe" and "receive." After this, we will focus on how depending on the events that surround these single word meanings will also help YOU overcome your desire to do self-harm or contemplate suicide. These simple words, their meanings and the events we are defining will provide you, as it has us, a great peace that simple sobriety could never afford!

BELIEVE

The word ***believe*** means, "to be persuaded to accept a truth through complete dependency upon it." The Bible tells us that Jesus is the Truth and anyone who knows this Truth will be made free. (See John 14:6 and John 8:32)

However, in order for Jesus' sacrifice to be applied to our personal sin debt, we must "be persuaded to accept this Truth of Jesus' death, burial, and resurrection through complete dependency upon it." When we are fully persuaded that something is true, we will depend upon that truth, that is to say, we will believe it!

Belief is another word for confidence or faith. But, your confidence in something must be accepted through a **complete dependence** upon the truth believed in order to qualify as real faith. In other words, in order to be saved, you must "completely depend on Jesus" as the payer of your sin debt through His DBR (death, burial, resurrection). We must have confidence in Him that leads us to depend on Him alone to save us from the debt we owe for our wrong doings in life.

With that said, we do not *need* to add good works, or join a church, or give money, or even "go to confession" to get to Heaven. We only depend on His DBR! That is what the Bible calls "saving faith." We must **believe** *on* Him in order to **receive** Him. Now, what do we receive when we believe on Him?

RECEIVE

Receive means "to obtain from another." The Bible tells us that if we will believe in our hearts that Jesus died on the cross and that God raised Him from the dead that we would be saved. (See Romans 10:9) When we are saved, our sin debt is paid and He gives to us eternal life. If you believe on Him, you will receive this from Him.

Eternal life is best defined as "life in perpetuity." This is to say, it is a life that begins when we get saved (or, are born again) and lasts forever. That is why we can commit to you that your new life will provide you power over the self-destructive path you are now on. It has for me and many others just like me.

Our eternal life cannot be taken from us. (See 1 John 5:1) It is a free gift that cannot be earned by doing good or be taken away by doing bad. It is yours, if you will only believe and receive. Should we? Oh, yes, we all should. Could we? Oh yes, we all could accept this free gift. But, would you? That is the most important question that you will ever answer.

Salvation also gives us the empowering of Internal Persuasion. When we receive Christ as our Savior, the Bible tells us that His Holy Spirit comes to live within us. (See Ezekiel 36:27.) He lives within our spirit in what the Bible calls our inner man. Within the inner man, your spirit and the Spirit of God can have fellowship one with another. This is where we find our ability to worship God and the ability to gain victory over our vices, including, of course, self-harm or suicide!

This is God's simple plan of salvation, benefit number one—justification. When we experience justification, we **have been saved** from the *penalty* of sin.

Would you like to believe and accept Jesus

Christ as your Savior? It is the first step to freedom from the power of sin, but it is the most important step. This is the step that grants us the freedom we all need from the *penalty* of sin. As a matter of fact, if you find escape from self-harm, suicidal attempts, and other life crippling addictions but die and go to hell, your sobriety will not have been worth it whatsoever.

Friend, I plead with you today to take this first step! Consider praying this simple prayer to God, meaning it from your heart. Saying this prayer is a way to declare to God that you are depending on Jesus Christ alone for your salvation. The words themselves will not save you. Only dependence (faith) on Jesus Christ can grant us our salvation!

PRAYER: "Father, I know that I am a sinner and my sins have separated me from you. I am truly wrong and deserve to be punished for it. But, do believe that your Son, Jesus Christ, died to pay my sin penalty. I believe that He was buried for three days and was resurrected from the dead by the power of the Holy Spirit. I believe Jesus is alive, and hears my prayers. I accept His payment for my sins and invite His Spirit to indwell me and empower me to overcome my wrong behaviors. In Jesus' Name I pray, Amen."

If you have prayed this prayer, you need to let another Christian know as soon as possible. Contact your RU leader, your RU director, the church pastor, or another Christian friend so that they can help you fully understand each part of this decision.

Your belief systems are changing, and if you have placed your full dependence upon Jesus to save you, you now have a Presence living within you that can give you the power to behave differently. In other words, now that you have changed just one of the ways you believed, you are now empowered to change the way you think. This simple step can forever change the way you act.

To overcome the world's many vices, this new relationship you have established with Jesus needs to be developed. This relationship is strengthened by the Power of the indwelling Holy Spirit. The more you know Jesus, not *about* Him, but the more you personally *know* Him, the more *freedom* you will experience over the wrong doings of which you have been forgiven. This personal relationship will set you, as it has us, on a pilgrimage toward the second benefit of your salvation, your sanctification.

CHAPTER SIX
Our Conformation Through Sanctification

After we have experienced the transformation of justification, we can soon see a developing Power source within us that gives us the ability to behave differently. This Power source is the indwelling Holy Spirit of God. He is real, though it may seem spooky when defined. His Spirit gives us the ability to do things we would never be able to do in our own power. Not just overcoming our addictions, but living a life that is pleasing to God and man, loving your family and others, serving unselfishly and becoming a person who gives of oneself to meet the needs of others. These are just some of the great things that will be produced when you conform into the image of God.

The word **conform** means "to be poured into a mold." The world naturally pours its inhabitants into a mold. At this stage of your life, you are conformed to this world's belief system, which, by the way, got you in the trouble you are in. But, the Bible tells us that God does not want us conformed to this world, but rather He wants us conformed

> "BEING RAISED AS A PASTOR'S KID, I WAS INSTRUCTED IN BIBLE KNOWLEDGE. BUT, I HAD TO CHOOSE, AS YOU DO, TO TAKE THAT KNOWLEDGE AND BEGIN TO KNOW JESUS IN A DYNAMIC, INTIMATE RELATIONSHIP." —DR. GEORGE CRABB

to the image of His Son Jesus Christ. (See Romans 12:2.) This takes place through a process that the Bible calls sanctification. Sanctification is the process whereby we actually develop a personal relationship with Jesus Christ, using the communication Tool of the indwelling Holy Spirit of God. At RU, we will help you understand not only the importance of this relationship, but also the simplicity of a dynamic love relationship with Jesus. At RU, our entire curriculum is designed to help you develop this relationship called sanctification.

Sanctification is the second of our three benefits in God's plan of salvation. Like justification, this takes place the moment we accept Jesus as our personal Savior. *Sanctification* means "to be set apart for sacred use." However, just because we are set apart for sacred use, does not mean that God is using all believers sacredly!

Many believers fail to disciple, or become students of Christ's. If we do not become students of Christ as disciples, we will never learn about Him. The information we will fail to gain will make it difficult for us to develop a relationship with Him. If we fail to enjoy the benefits of our sanctification, we will seldom enjoy the power of God on our lives!

Failing to develop a walk with Christ is the wrong way for a believer to live their new Christian life. If you make this mistake too, you will fail to overcome many different sins in your life, especially the **SELF-HARM** or **SUICIDAL THOUGHTS** that brought you to our program.

At Reformers Unanimous, our program focus is on developing our students to enjoy the benefits of their sanctification. Our students consist of newborn believers and long-time believers that are discouraged and apathetic Christians. We help these students obtain their walk with God through our intense discipleship curriculum, effective and motivational classes, individual, personal and group counseling, navigational principles that lead to prosperity in life, and active participation in church related events. All of the personal development we invest in the students of RU is free of charge. The only charge at RU is for cost of the books you may *choose* to purchase.

During our class time, we are instructed to develop as our goals the following eight "ships" as our system for overcoming the power that our addictions have gained over us:

>**Worship**–humbling oneself in order to exalt God in personal praise.
>
>**Discipleship**–learning how God acts, how man acts, and how man acts when he is trying to act like God in his own power.
>
>**Relationship**–developing intimacy through a daily *talk* with God that produces a day-long *walk* with God.
>
>**Fellowship**–an association between people of like faith that we may enjoy the stability that comes from accountability.
>
>**Followship**–placing our life's most important decisions and choices under the influence of our God-ordained leadership, our umbrella of protection.

Leadership–placing our time and talents under the jurisdictional oversight of our God-ordained leaders.

Stewardship–placing our tithe (to be explained later) where God demands and our treasures where God directs.

Apprenticeship–learning from a personal Spirit-filled trainer how to love God, love others, and to serve God and others out of an appreciation for that great love.

Each of these "ships" are developmental stages. They are detailed in the Reformers Unanimous book, <u>Eight Ships That Shape Your Ship—Shipshape!</u> You can order this important book and many other RU materials at your chapter book table, church bookstore or online at **www.rurecovery.com**.

In this small, spiritual booklet on **SELF-HARM** and **SUICIDE**, it would be difficult to explain all that a believer needs to understand concerning the sanctification process. However, we will attempt to explain sanctification in this chapter as an overview of its many benefits to your new-found faith.

Please remember that sanctification is a lifelong process of aligning every part of your soul and body with the indwelling Spirit of the living God. This DOES NOT take incredible work on our part. Rather, it takes an intimate walk where you and He seldom part!! This walk with the Christ that saved our soul will grant us the Power over any bad habits we may have in our life.

You see, when we first began to dabble with sinful vices, they did not bind us. They seldom even restricted us. They were enjoyable and satisfying in the many ways listed in chapter three. But, over the course of time, it began the process of becoming a stubborn habit. That stubborn habit is now a full-fledged addiction that is in the process of taking your whole world away from you. It was a four step process that placed you in this position.

Your addiction began as a **TOEHOLD**. As a toehold, it was a bit of an inconvenience at times, but did not really slow you down too much. The enjoyment was worth the nagging sensation you often felt the next day. However, as you fed that appetite, it only grew stronger. An appetite once fed never grows weaker. It only grows stronger.

Eventually this habit grew to be a **FOOTHOLD**. As a foothold, it slowed your progress. You didn't seem to advance as quickly or recover as fast from the mistakes this habit was causing you to make.

However, you still advanced, albeit awkwardly, and you still recovered. But, eventually, your foothold became a **STRONGHOLD**. As a stronghold, it has become, well, just that—something that has a strong hold on you. As a stronghold, it not only slows your progress, but it also slows your productivity, like a pair of handcuffs would. You are not as productive in your personal life or your professional life and everything begins to fall apart.

It is at this stage that most of our students reach out to our "out-patient" local church addictions program for help. They are still functioning in society, but barely. They are losing jobs, experiencing failed marriages and their homes are often broken at this stage. It is sad when they are at this point in their life for often they are just beginning to look for help. But, it is a very difficult process to find freedom on your own. I believe it

> "THESE FOUR STAGES ARE ILLUSTRATED AS AN "INFECTIOUS" PROCESS. A SKIN INFECTION STARTS AS A MICROSCOPIC INVASION, THEN SPREADS TO SURROUNDING SKIN, THEN INTO THE DEEPER TISSUE, AND FINALLY INFILTRATES INTO THE BLOOD SYSTEM WHERE IT CAN NOW DESTROY THE WHOLE BODY."
> —DR. GEORGE CRABB

is nearly impossible. Without Jesus you may find sobriety, but you will not find contentment in the difficult journey of life.

However, some reject the solutions that many programs offer them and carry on with their addictive habits until the addiction develops from a stronghold into a full blown **STRANGLEHOLD**. A stranglehold will takes us wherever it wants us to go and restricts us from going anywhere we may want to go. Though a stronghold will bind you, a stranglehold will enslave you. It will control your entire life's existence. You live to feed it, and if you don't feed it, you will begin to think you are going to die!

At the stranglehold stage, you are a non-functioning addict. At this point, you will probably need a full-time residential program. This is the stage we find most of our applicants to our men's and women's residential Schools of Discipleship homes in Rockford, IL. The folks in our homes are barely functioning and they CANNOT find freedom unless they leave behind their troubled environment.

Our residential Schools of Discipleship (**www.ruhomes.org**) is a program that acts like a green house. It protects an addict from their environment so that they can grow really fast. If this is where you find yourself, please understand that those whose addiction appears to have a stranglehold on them will find great help at RU and the church that hosts it, but it may be necessary to take a break for a period of months in your life and recover from the snare in which you have found yourself.

With these four stages of addiction understood, we can see how sanctification is not the only lifelong process. Your personal destruction has been developing for a great portion of your life, as well. The moment we begin to rebel as young men or women against the authority system that God designed, we began a journey that leads to our eventual ruin. For me, that ruin emanated from addictive, sinful habits that I formed as a young man in rebellion to my parent's wishes.

For most people with addiction problems, it has taken a long time to develop these bad habits. It will take some time as well until your spiritual development will be strong enough to overcome those habits. However, most of our students see great victory almost instantaneously and experience lasting victory shortly thereafter. Why? Because in the process of sanctification, it is God that does the work, not the recovering addict.

With that said, God intends for our recovery process to begin at conversion through the justification of our soul and the sanctification of our spirit. God intends for the benefits of sanctification to begin at our conversion to Christ and to be increasing in enjoyment throughout the remainder of our lifetime. In justification, we are "made right in heaven." Sanctification is how we become "more right on earth."

When we accept by faith God's simple plan of salvation, we are entitled to the benefits of sanctification. The primary benefit of justification is freedom from the *penalty of sin* but the primary benefit of sanctification is freedom from the *power of sin*. The benefits that come from submitting to God's process of sanctification is what leads us to the abundant life that Jesus promised to those who would live their life IN Christ Jesus.

To best explain how sanctification grants us His Power over sin and thus neutralizes the need to overcome sinful addictions in our own power, we will look at the **same six key words** that we defined in our last chapter. Each of these words that we defined in justification will be used to define both sanctification and glorification, as well.

SIN

Do Christians commit sin? The Bible tells us that after we are justified, we are now "made right in heaven". But, that does not make us automatically able to live right on earth. It is not by my power or might that I can avoid sinning, but by His Spirit that I can remain free from the power of sin. (See Zechariah 4:6.)

But, as believers, the issue is no longer whether or not we *commit* sin, but rather whether or not we willingly *permit* sin. (See First John 3:9.) Let me explain what that means. God has given every believer access to His Spirit of Power over the dormant power of sin that remains in our bodies. This wonder-working Power is harnessed within my inner man in the form of God's Holy Spirit. Wrong desires from outside pressure (temptations and trials) after my conversion continue to stimulate my mind to think wrong thoughts. But, it is when my mind chooses to *submit* to that stimulation that I have made the choice to *permit* sin. (See Romans 7:15-17.)

In others words, before we ever *do* wrong, we FIRST choose to *think* wrong! Thus, we do wrong before we actually *did* wrong, if you know what I mean. So, you can see that as Christians, it is not so much that we are sin *committers*. It is that we are choosing first to be sin *permitters*!

The Bible clearly teaches us that if we will not *permit* sin to enter into our thought processes, we will not *commit* those sins. Thus, the Power of

God's Spirit is necessary to keep those thoughts from becoming constant daily meditations. (See Proverbs 23:7a.) If we think them, we will enter into unnecessary temptations that, if not handled properly, will lead us back to our addictive, sinful habits.

DEATH

Thinking wrong is a weakness of both the saved and the lost. But, it is the saved who have been given a guaranteed way of escape WITH the bad thoughts. (See First Corinthians 10:13.) Whenever outside pressure (oppression) stimulates our mind to think wrong, a discipled and developed Internal Presence from God will influence us to reject that outside pressure to sin. This "way of escape" will be provided WITH the temptation. Thus, at the same time we are tempted to think wrong, there is an exit ramp in our mind to get off the "road to eventual ruin." If we reject His "way of escape," we will pass by it and be forced to deal with the temptation in our own power. That is to say, we will have to find our own way of escape. Only our strong character can help us at this stage. And, if our will power is weak, we will probably soon commit that sin in our body, for we have permitted that sin to dwell in our mind. (See James 1:14-15)

In order to take the "way of escape" that the Power of His Presence provides, we must be willing to experience a death to self at the moment of His prompting in order to exit this road of ruin. We must literally be willing to **die to self** every day, and throughout the day. To die to self means to reject our selfish desires to think wrong.

So, we see that even as Christ died for us, we must also now be willing to **die *with* Christ**. (See Romans 6:6)

At Reformers Unanimous, our discipleship curriculum will teach you how you may experience that daily death that is a prerequisite for obtaining what the Bible calls the "Power of His resurrection." His Power can work through the life of a flawed man, but His Power works best through the life of a dead man! That is to say, a man that dies to his own selfishness.

BURIAL

When we die to self out of an unselfish desire to obey His promptings, we will experience a satisfaction of sorts. For we learn that when we suffer loss that we enjoy closer fellowship with Him. (See Philippians 3:8 and 10.) This period of intimate "fellowship of His suffering" represents our time of burial. Metaphorically, as we wait for God to empower us to get through a difficult situation, we are in a dormant position. We are dead to our own wishes but not yet alive in His Power. At this time, we are metaphorically secluded from the outside world and its ways, but we have a work going on with Christ in the darkness of our inner man.

This process, which I call our "time in the tomb" precedes the power that comes from His resurrected Life living through us. You may not understand this right now or quite see the symbolism of what I am teaching you, but as you grow and mature IN Christ through our addictions program, these truths will become real and personal to you.

So, we see that the Bible tells us that we are not only crucified *with* Christ as we die to self, but that we are also buried *with* Christ as He destroys the influences that want to control us. (See Romans 6:4) This time of waiting for His power is designed to be a sweet time of rest. But, for many believers, it is rejected and becomes, instead, a time of turbulent wrest.

At Reformers Unanimous, we will teach you through our discipleship curriculum how to patiently wait in your proverbial tomb as that which is "on your mind" may be starved of thought and eventually dissolve from your heart's meditation. When that wrong thought is no longer actively at work in your meditation, the enemy can no longer use it as a tool of manipulation. This allows you to experience the transformation process that grants you the Christ life that comes from His resurrection.

RESURRECTION

Sometimes we circumvent the resurrection process of the Christ Life when we choose to wrest *with* Christ rather than rest *in* Christ. We wrestle *with* Christ when, after we willingly die to self, but because of a difficult circumstance, we impatiently reject our time of waiting in the tomb for His power to come upon us. We, thus, yield to our own devices in order to overcome life's troubles. (See Proverbs 14:12)

We have died WITH Christ. We are buried WITH Christ and He intends for us to patiently await His timetable in order for us to be risen WITH Christ. (See Romans 6:4-5)

At Reformers Unanimous, we will teach you through our training and discipleship curriculum how to patiently wait on the Lord to renew your strength. This process of waiting on Him will surely give us the power that RU promises is available to us to overcome our stubborn habits and addictions. This is a truth you must believe if you are going to see any lasting change take place IN you.

BELIEVE

It takes belief, that is to say, faith, to save us.

But, it also takes faith to change us. Before we are saved, we have very little faith. After we are saved, we are given the "faith of Christ" as one of the nine Fruit of the Holy Spirit. (See Galatians 5:22)

The term "Hidden life" is the daily death from our own affections and lusts in order to experience the Spirit Life. The Spirit Life comes from patiently resting in state for His Power to perform a good work in us. It is when we are "Hid-IN-Life."

To engage in this Hidden Life, we must exercise more dependence on Him than what it took to save us. But, this is not an increased dependence that is quantitive. For dependence is dependence. But, rather, it is an increased dependence that is durative. The duration (or length) of our faith is longer and longer between our "bouts with doubt." This increase of duration in our trust IN Him takes place as we spiritually develop. But, it is not *our* faith in which we are learning to remain confident. It is *His* faith that I must submit myself unto in order to experience the benefits of my sanctification. It takes my faith IN Christ to save me, but it takes *the* faith OF Christ to change me. (See Galatians 2:20 and Philippians 3:9.)

At Reformers Unanimous, our goal is to develop you out of your unbelief. There are many things that our human minds do not immediately comprehend. But, His faith that dwells within our spirit must operate independent of our feelings which dwell within our soul. When we know that God says something is true, we must accept it with the faith that He has placed within us. We cannot do this without a relationship IN Him. At RU, our discipleship curriculum will help you develop that intimate and abiding love relationship with Jesus Christ. If you will believe *in* Him, you receive *from* Him.

RECEIVE

Jesus said that He came that we might have life, and that we might have it more abundantly. (See John 10:10) When we refuse to die *with* Christ, or to lie *with* Christ, or to rise *with* Christ, then our Christian life will be up and down, at best. That is not the *abundant* life; that is the *redundant* life. I want to receive what God has given unto me—eternal life. That life begins at conversion.

But, in order to enjoy eternal life before I get to heaven, I must be willing to *do* as Christ *did*. Die, be buried, and be raised to walk in newness of life. (See Romans 6:4) If I yield to His faith in me, then I will receive His life living through me.

When we receive Christ as our Savior, the Holy Spirit will begin to persuade us through intuition, conviction, and worship. Whenever we reject any aspect of our selfless death, patient burial, and empowered resurrection, we stunt that internal persuasion and hinder our ability to live holy (soberly, righteously, and godly) in this present world. (See Titus 2:12) This will not separate us from God's presence, but it will strain His persuasion over us. We remain sanctified (set apart), but we no longer enjoy the benefits of our sanctification—abundant life, free from the power of sin and addiction.

At Reformers Unanimous, we *do not* help **addicts** live free from sin and addiction. We help **Christians** free live from sin and addiction. If you are a Christian, we believe this program can be a great help to you.

However, for RU to be of service to anyone,

one must be willing to continue in this lifelong process of changing the way that we think. At RU, our goal is to help us overcome our "stinkin' thinking" by teaching everyone the biblical way to "tinker with your thinker."

At RU, we want to walk *with* you in our pilgrimage through sanctification. Together we will spiritually develop so that we may overcome all our crippling and habitual sins. Doing so brings us to our final chapter and benefit of salvation—glorification.

With our justification, we have BEEN saved from the PENALTY of sin. With our sanctification, we are BEING saved from the POWER of sin. Our third benefit is the future benefit of glorification. In glorification we shall BE saved from the PRESENCE of sin.

CHAPTER SEVEN
Our Reformation Through Glorification

This final benefit of glorification is the potential to glorify God in this life and the privilege to be glorified by God in the life hereafter. Our chapter title explains that we will be "reformed' thru glorification. Reformed is a key word at Reformers Unanimous, for it makes up the first word in our program's name.

Webster's dictionary defines the word *reform* to mean "to change from worse to better; to bring from a bad to a good state; to improve corrupt manners or morals, to remove that which is bad or corrupt; as, to reform abuses and to reform from vices."

That is a long definition that teaches us what God intends to do in our life. At RU, we hope to assist you in that process whereby God will "change you in more ways than just one." RU does not only focus on developing you from a drug addict to a sober living citizen, though we will focus on your recovery.

At RU, we want to help you experience much

more change that that! We want to see you go from being unsaved to saved. We want you to go from headed to Hell to being Heaven-bound! We want you to go from being a self-focused person to a person focused on others. Yes, and we want you to go from being a bad person to a good person.

This is a process whereby we focus on our spiritual development as well as our personal development. The process of spiritual development has been explained in the previous two chapters of this book. It will also be taught more thoroughly as you engage in our Strongholds Discipleship Program curriculum. In this chapter however, we want to discuss the level of personal development that should follow your Strongholds Course work. The graduate's course work at RU is entitled, "Gaining Remaining Fruit." It is a focus on developing any missing character qualities you may not have in your life. Character qualities are necessary building blocks that God intends for us to learn as children. But, for some people, they fail to have them taught or they have rejected them till much later in life. We want to help you "reform" your character, where needed, from bad to good.

The second word in our program name is "unanimous." The word *unanimous* means "being of one mind." What that means is that at RU we are all unanimously focused on one thing—change! But, it is not a change that is acquired in our own effort, but it is a change that is granted to us by God, through His Spirit for Jesus' sake. We all strive for the mind of Christ. It is this mind that should be within us all. (See Philippians 2:5)

This change requires only one thing from us—a two-fold belief. A confession that believes *on* Jesus through His blood for our justification to save us and a conviction to believe *in* Jesus through His Spirit for our sanctification to change us. When we accept these commitments and believe with all our heart, lasting change is the natural result. That is when the glorification of God begins.

The word *glory* means to "bring the right opinion of." It literally means to "make God look good." The day will come when we will be saved not only from the penalty of sin (our justification), not only from the power of sin (our sanctification), but also from the presence of sin (our glorification). Until the day we enter

Heaven's gate, our focus should not be on OUR glorification but rather on HIS glorification!

The Bible tells us that everything God created was intended to bring Him glory, to make Him look good. That is not the goal of many people's lives today, but God wants that to be our goal. We should strive to meet that goal by trusting in Him to reform us into God-glorifying new creatures in Christ.

With that said, sanctification is the key to glorification. If you are developing a dynamic love relationship with Jesus Christ, you will glorify God in your life. However, there will be times when your walk is weak or the adversity is particularly strong. We like to say at RU that "new levels bring new devils." At times like this, if we don't have strong character to lean on in spiritually weak times, we will be tempted to do things that may eventually lead us back to our addictive behavior. We may not "use" right away, but if we are not quick to make it right with God, we may grow farther from Him and engage in our sins of choice shortly thereafter.

During this process, which is called spiritual

backsliding, we will need to have developed some character if we are going to remain *doing* right as we strive to *get* right. Now, please be advised that strong character is no substitute for strong Christianity. But, without strong character, we will be powerless when God's power is not granted to us.

Most addicts have character in some areas, but lack character in other areas. For example, you may have strong character traits like punctuality, initiative, good work ethic, or attentiveness. But, you may struggle in other areas like rebellion to authority, selfishness, pride, laziness, or jealousy. You can't glorify God especially during difficult times in your life if your weak character fails to improve. Your frustrations will overwhelm you and you will not do right unless circumstances change.

God may not want your circumstances to change. In Christ, you don't have to do right, you just have to submit to desiring to do right, then He does the work for you. However, if we are not abiding IN Christ, we are not right with God. It takes character to *do* right when you are not right.

At times like this, you are the one doing right. This is not God's choice, but it is better than doing wrong. It won't produce joy, but it will keep you from the consequences of sins done in the body. So, character development is important, especially for those who have very little.

However, the Bible says the Spirit of God WILL "sustain your infirmities." That word ***infirmities*** means "weaknesses." Our indwelling Spirit is strong enough to help us overcome our character weaknesses, even though we may remain personally insufficient to do so in our own power. At RU, we want you to learn to overcome those personal weaknesses as well as spiritually develop. It is designed for your own personal development.

This effort is made on your part by engaging in our graduate's course curriculum. We have two courses for our students. The entry level course is entitled "Strongholds," which is focused on developing the "fruits of the Spirit," which produces "righteousness." But, the graduate's course is entitled, "Gaining Remaining Fruit," which is focused on developing the "fruits of righteousness," which is godly Christian character.

This course is designed to help you determine which missing character qualities might drift you back into your addiction during particularly difficult times in your spiritual pilgrimage.

Again, it is important that you understand that any character qualities we may fail to develop as young people are now of secondary importance to being a good Christian. Many people have good character but they may not be good Christians. We only glorify God when people see the strength of our Spirit, not the strength of our soul. In other words, we cannot exhibit the glorification of God to others without first enjoying the benefits of the sanctification of His Spirit—that is to say the benefits that come from developing an intimate personal relationship with Christ. Those benefits are the fruit (which means, "outcome or result") of the Spirit: love, joy, peace, longsuffering, gentleness, goodness, faith, meekness, and temperance.

So, we see that in order for our life to bring God glory right now, we must first focus on developing ourselves spiritually. Now at the same time, God will work on developing our personal lives to become stronger. This combination will be the best way to *stay* strong lest you *stray* weak!

At RU, we look forward to the opportunity of assisting you to spiritually develop first and foremost, and to personally develop you thereafter. However, someday there will be an even better experience for you my friend; and that is eternal glorification!

Someday all believers will glorify God in EVERYTHING that we do FOREVERMORE! The word *glorification* means almost the same thing as glory, or glorify. It means "to exalt One in honor and esteem." Someday, all believers will be exalted to a position where we will ALWAYS bring God honor and esteem. That day will come upon our physical death or His eminent return to earth in what the Bible calls "the rapture." Your RU leadership can explain what that means to you. It will be the most exciting time of your life, I can promise you that.

To date, all but two people who have gone into Heaven have done so as a result of their own physical death. In other words, they have died and awoken in Heaven, so to speak. When a believer's physical life ends, their body dies and their soul enters into Heaven's abode where they will forever bring Him glory.

When we accept God's simple plan of salvation, He does give us the power we need to glorify Him with our lives. It is even God's purpose for leaving us here for so long after our conversions—that others might see Him IN us and believe on His name. This brings God great glory here on earth.

But, from time to time, our lack of faith during particularly difficult times will lead us into failure in certain areas of our lives. At times like this, we will fail to glorify God. Likewise, we will be a disappointment to ourselves.

You see, the Power we need to glorify God comes from being completely yielded to Him. Remaining completely and unequivocally yielded to God is impossible when sin's presence is still alive in our bodies and actively trying to influence our lives.

However, when we are "lifted up to heaven," we will FINALLY experience freedom from the *presence of sin*. This future benefit grants us the sinless perfection that God originally designed for each of us to enjoy. In order to explain how to glorify God here on earth and how the glorification of God in Heaven actually works, allow me to use the same key words that we explained in our chapters on *Transformation Through Justification* and *Conformation Through Sanctification*.

SIN

When we are glorifying God, it is because sin has no dominion over us at a particular time. Its power has been rendered useless for we have chosen to die to the selfish desires of our soul and to yield to the depth of the personal relationship we have established in Christ through faith.

This means that the grace of God has taken over our life and is giving us the power to cast down the imaginations that usually stimulate us to yield to a particular temptation. This is not a once-for-all experience. When we allow our faith to waver to a form of doubt or blatant unbelief in Him, then our relationship suffers and adversity will be much harder to overcome.

Our improved character may keep us from

outwardly sinning or even quickly sinning. But, eventually, if we do no rectify the mistakes we are making in our walk with God, then our character will grow weak. This will leave us vulnerable to the internal sin of wrong thinking. Once again, this wrong thinking is found in the meditations of our heart.

Shortly after our wrong meditations begin we will probably give into this contemplation of temptation. When this happens, we will not glorify God for we are no longer under His power. Thus we cannot maintain a righteous lifestyle. It is impossible to live godly in our own power.

This compromise leads us to *permit* sinful thoughts in our mind to overcome the meditations of our heart. Once we permit ourselves to think about sin with any lengthy duration whatsoever, it will eventually cause us to *commit* that sin in our body. It was earlier explained that, when we permit sin to control our heart, we are already engaging in wrong behavior. Thus we will soon commit that wrong. But, we have already permitted ourselves to *being* wrong before we commit ourselves to *doing* wrong. To "be holy" we must give our minds over to God. To "be unholy" we must give our minds over to the things of this world.

This internal permitting of sin in our mind is what separates us from fellowship with God and hinders the Spirit's ability to glorify God with our life. That is how sin will stunt our ability to glorify God here on earth.

However, when Christ shall come, all believers shall see a change take place "in the air." That change will eradicate our sin nature. This means that when we enter heaven, we will have been forever saved from the *presence* of sin. Once again, this rapture really should be explained to you by your RU leader.

DEATH

There are two types of death that lead to glorification. One type of death glorifies God and the other will bring us glorification. Let's first look at the death that brings glory to God. We have discussed it earlier, as well. It is the death of self. When we commit ourselves to dying to oneself and choose rather to live by the prompting of our indwelling Holy Spirit, we are experiencing the benefits of conforming through our sanctification. Some believers do that often, others sometimes, and some hardly ever. Those who rarely die to self do not bring glory to God. Even when they are able to do right, those who know them best recognize it as a seldom experienced victory and will be skeptical of their good works. This will not glorify God. They know the person well enough to know they cannot maintain the consistency that comes only from dying daily to our own selfish wants.

So, God may receive a small measure of glory, but it soon fades as that person falls back into their fleshly, stubborn ways. This is not the type of occasional dying experience that God wants from us. He wants us to die to self every day, throughout the day.

But, we are unable to do so unless we develop a deep abiding relationship with Jesus Christ that manifests itself in wanting what He wants, thinking like He thinks, and feeling the way He feels. We need to nurture our nature to be more like Christ, not by changing our life but by exchanging our life for His life!

The Bible says that when we are crucified spiritually we are crucified WITH Christ. Though we are still alive physically, it is Him that has come to life spiritually. Thus, it is Christ that is supposed to be living His life within me. The Bible says that Christ living in me is the hope of glory. The word *hope* means "expectation." The only expectation I have for bringing God glory is for Christ to live IN me that I may submit to allowing Him to live FOR me. That is the "hid-in-life" we teach at RU.

To bring God glory, not once for a little while, but regularly for long periods, we need to die to self, as prompted by God. This takes a commitment to following the Spirit's leading while learning how to "walk after the Spirit." This is how we glorify God with our lives. It is the Christ Life being accessed through our own personal death to the self life.

However, if we physically perish before Christ returns, then upon our death, it is our human body that experiences death. If we are believers, as outlined in our chapter on transformation thru justification, our soul will never die. Our soul has been spared its much deserved death as a result of our accepting Christ payment on the cross. (See James 5:20.)

Though our body parts will cease to function and we will be buried as we experience our physical death, the soul is incorruptible, it never dies. Our soul will take on immortality in a perfect state as promised by God in His Word. (See First Corinthians 15:53.)

This death will bring US glorification, which once again, is freedom from the presence of sin. However, after our spiritual daily death or our physical once-in-a-lifetime death, there will be a time of burial.

BURIAL

When we die to our selfish wants and wishes, we will be at a proverbial crossroads. At this stage we can climb off that cross as a dead man and resurrect our lives in our power and begin "trying hard to do better." But, if we do this, we will only fail again and again with no real sign of victory. Or, we can patiently wait for God's power to come upon us before we advance down the right path at that crossroads. The timing of our outside pressure to *do* wrong and our internal persuasion to *be* right comes simultaneously. But, as a result of a weakened walk, the internal persuasion is easily overlooked.

This ought not to be. The Bible says a wise man see evil coming and hides himself from it. But, naive people pass on and receive a punishment for the error of their ways. If we are going to glorify God with our lives, we must be willing to die and remain buried until Christ resurrects Himself in us. The Apostle Paul (one of the men that God used to pen the words of the Bible) said he died daily, but he never said he resurrected daily. For it was not him that resurrected but rather it was Him!

RESURRECTION

Though we may wrestle with Christ in our own power and have a tendency during times of weak faith to falter as a result, God is faithful to not suffer us to be tempted with more than we can handle. As a result, our stubbornness when being unselfish will bring us great conviction or even adversity that is clearly the chastening of the Lord. At this time, we are more willing to "get it over with" and die spiritually that we may resurrect with Him. If we take this process through its supernatural course, then we will patently wait for His indwelling Spirit to lead us out of our mistakes. This is our spiritual resurrection. It is our stubborn soul dying, and our developing spirit resurrecting and taking its rightful role of authority over our thoughts, wishes, and wants.

This process brings God *great* glory for at times like this we are humbling ourselves! Bold humility (Boldness is faith, and humility is trust in God rather than oneself) is the key to gaining grace and mercy in our times of need. (See Hebrews 4:16)

This humbling process will keep us from returning so quickly to the self reliance that brings us back to a position of pride. Returning back to our position of pride is what brings us to another painful crucifixion. Though a crucifixion for our wrong wishes brings God glory, nothing glorifies Him more than when our submission to His Spirit reveals to others a desire to abide deeper IN Him.

When we die or Christ returns, we will forever be glorified and free from the presence of sin. God's creation will once again function as He had created it in the beginning. Until that glorious day, we ought always to glorify God and not our own selves. This can only be done as we reject sin's *pressure* in our life and yield to God's *power* over sin's presence. This takes only submission to what we have chosen to believe during difficult circumstances.

BELIEVE

My friend, have you believed that Jesus Christ can transform your life thorough the salvation experience of justification? If so, you are born again and you have BEEN saved from the PENALTY of sin, which is death and Hell.

If you have been saved through the faith found in justification, have you also chosen to begin a relationship with Him in which you are learning to follow His leading? If you are doing so, or are committed to do so, then my friend, you are BEING saved from the POWER of sin.

And, finally, are you committed to having a long-term walk with God by yielding yourself to that developing relationship with God's Son through His Spirit? If you do this with regularity and reject compromise in your thought life, then my friend, you will bring God great glory in this life. You have been reformed by your desires to make Him look good with your life!

Your next and final benefit remains to be seen. It will be the day and time when you and I and Dr. Crabb and many untold others will be glorified. It is at that time we will BE saved from the PRESENCE of sin. Until that day, I ask of God that peace be with you. Not a temporary peace that any program may be able to grant you, but the "Peace that passes understanding". It comes only from God as we enjoy and experience all the benefits of your salvation.

The Transformation of Justification: Have you **been saved** from sin's *penalty*? If not, then you need to be justified. If you have been justified, then you will be **judged as a** child of God and saved from sin's *penalty*.

The Conformation of Sanctification: Are you also **being saved** from sin's *power*? If not, then you need to enjoy the primary benefit that comes from sanctification. It is a deep abiding personal relationship with Him that manifests itself in victory over vice. We will make mistakes and find ourselves being **judged as a son**. However, God will develop us like the loving Father He is to be the son we never thought we could be. This development will save us regularly from sin's *power*.

The Reformation of Glorification: Are you victorious in life, enjoying the abundant Christian life? If so, then you are avoiding the disruption that can be caused by sin's presence in the members of your body. That is to be commended. However, the day will come when we will all be **judged as a servant**. How did we serve others? This will take place after our glorification when we **will be saved** from sin's *presence*.

I know that not all of these truths will be easily or even immediately understood by all who read this book. Very few will have even heard a great many of the facts found in this book, backed up by the Scriptures found in the back of the book. However, that doesn't matter. If you are willing and wanting to learn more about the Truth, He will be revealed to you at a pace that God feels is appropriate for you.

Right now, you may receive from God what the Bible refers to as the "milk of the Word." But, His Word teaches us that as we use it regularly, we will mature to what the Bible calls "strong meat." The truths taught in this book may start as milk and become quite meaty. Worry not. We at RU are here to help you on this journey. And, when your pilgrimage is over, you will be quite pleased with what God has done for you.

In conclusion, I surely hope you will study this book over and over again. And, if you visited one of our chapters recently, we hope to see you again next week.

SCRIPTURE REFERENCE

Proverbs 14:12 *There is a way which seemeth right unto a man, but the end thereof are the ways of death.*

Proverbs 23:7a *For as he thinketh in his heart, so is he.*

Ezekiel 36:27 *And I will put my spirit within you, and cause you to walk in my statutes, and ye shall keep my judgments, and do them.*

Zechariah 4:6 *Then he answered and spake unto me, saying, This is the word of the LORD unto Zerubbabel, saying, Not by might, nor by power, but by my spirit, saith the LORD of hosts.*

Matthew 27:62 *Now the next day, that followed the day of the preparation, the chief priests and Pharisees came together unto Pilate,*

Matthew 27:63 *Saying, Sir, we remember that that deceiver said, while he was yet alive, After three days I will rise again.*

Matthew 27:64 *Command therefore that the sepulchre be made sure until the third day, lest his disciples come by night, and steal him away, and say unto the people, He is risen from the dead: so the last error shall be worse than the first.*

Matthew 27:65 *Pilate said unto them, Ye have a watch: go your way, make it as sure as ye can.*

Matthew 28:5 *And the angel answered and said unto the women, Fear not ye: for I know that ye seek Jesus, which* was *crucified.*

Matthew 28:6 *He is not here: for he is risen, as he said. Come, see the place where the Lord lay.*

Matthew 28:7 *And go quickly, and tell his disciples that he is risen from the dead; and, behold, he goeth before you into Galilee; there shall ye see him: lo, I have told you.*

John 3:16 *For God so loved the world, that he gave his only begotten Son, that whosoever believeth in him should not perish, but have everlasting life.*

John 8:32 *And ye shall know the truth, and the truth shall make you free.*

John 8:36 *If the Son therefore shall make you free, ye shall be free indeed.*

John 10:10 *The thief cometh not, but for to steal, and to kill, and to destroy: I am come that they might have life, and that they might have it more abundantly.*

John 14:16 *And I will pray the Father, and he shall give you another Comforter, that he may abide with you for ever;*

Romans 3:23 *For all have sinned, and come short of the glory of God;*

Romans 5:8 *But God commendeth his love toward us, in that, while we were yet sinners, Christ died for us.*

Romans 5:12 *Wherefore, as by one man sin entered into the world, and death by sin; and so death passed upon all men, for that all have sinned:*

Romans 6:4 *Therefore we are buried with him by baptism into death: that like as Christ was raised up from the dead by the glory of the Father, even so we also should walk in newness of life.*

Romans 6:5 *For if we have been planted together in the likeness of his death, we shall be also in the likeness of his resurrection:*

Romans 6:6 *Knowing this, that our old man is crucified with him, that the body of sin might be destroyed, that henceforth we should not serve sin.*

Romans 6:23 *For the wages of sin is death; but the gift of God is eternal life through Jesus Christ our Lord.*

Romans 7:15 *For that which I do I allow not: for what I would, that do I not; but what I hate, that do I.*

Romans 7:16 *If then I do that which I would not, I consent unto the law that it is good.*

Romans 7:17 *Now then it is no more I that do it, but sin that dwelleth in me.*

Romans 10:9 *That if thou shalt confess with thy mouth the Lord Jesus, and shalt believe in thine heart that God hath raised him from the dead, thou shalt be saved.*

Romans 12:2 *And be not conformed to this world: but be ye transformed by the renewing of your mind, that ye may prove what is that good, and acceptable, and perfect, will of God.*

1Corinthians 10:13 *There hath no temptation taken you but such as is common to man: but God is faithful, who will not suffer you to be tempted above that ye are able; but will with the temptation also make a way to escape, that ye may be able to bear it.*

1Corinthians 15:53 *For this corruptible must put on incorruption, and this mortal must put on immortality.*

Galatians 2:20 *I am crucified with Christ: nevertheless I live; yet not I, but Christ liveth in me: and the life which I now live in the flesh I live by the faith of the Son of God, who loved me, and gave himself for me.*

Galatians 5:22 *But the fruit of the Spirit is love, joy, peace, longsuffering, gentleness, goodness, faith.*

Philippians 3:8 *Yea doubtless, and I count all things but loss for the excellency of the knowledge of Christ Jesus my Lord: for whom I have suffered the loss of all things, and do count them but dung, that I may win Christ,*

Philippians 3:9 *And be found in him, not having mine own righteousness, which is of the law, but that which is through the faith of Christ, the righteousness which is of God by faith:*

Philippians 3:10 *That I may know him, and the power of his resurrection, and the fellowship of his sufferings, being made conformable unto his death;*

Titus 2:12 *Teaching us that, denying ungodliness and worldly lusts, we should live soberly, righteously, and godly, in this present world;*

Hebrews 4:16 *Let us therefore come boldly unto the throne of grace, that we may obtain mercy, and find grace to help in time of need.*

James 1:14 *But every man is tempted, when he is drawn away of his own lust, and enticed.*

James 1:15 *Then when lust hath conceived, it bringeth forth sin: and sin, when it is finished, bringeth forth death.*

James 5:20 *Let him know, that he which converteth the sinner from the error of his way shall save a soul from death, and shall hide a multitude of sins.*

1 Peter 3:18 *For Christ also hath once suffered for sins, the just for the unjust, that he might bring us to God, being put to death in the flesh, but quickened by the Spirit:*

1 John 3:9 *Whosoever is born of God doth not commit sin; for his seed remaineth in him: and he cannot sin, because he is born of God.*

1 John 5:1 *Whosoever believeth that Jesus is the Christ is born of God: and every one that loveth him that begat loveth him also that is begotten of him.*

Dr. George T. Crabb, D.O.
Certified Internal Medicine Doctor
Member of American Society of Addiction Medicine

Dr. Crabb is a long-standing member of Antioch Baptist Church in Warren, Michigan, where his father is the founder and pastor. He is an ordained minister and holds the office of Chairman of the Deacon Board. Dr. Crabb also teaches an adult Sunday school class and serves as Superintendent of Antioch Baptist Academy.

Dr. George Crabb is board certified in internal medicine. He served at the Physician Medical office in Rochester Hills, Michigan, William Beaumont Hospital, and St. John Oakland Affiliation. He is a member of the American Society of Addiction Medicine.

Steve Boyd Curington
October 1, 1965-October 30, 2010
Founder of RU Recovery Ministries

Steve grew up in Rockford, Illinois, and attended North Love Christian School. Upon graduation, Steve walked away from the truths he had learned and thus began a 10 year drug addiction. After a serious car accident, Steve was delivered from his addiction through the support of North Love Baptist Church.

Because of his new found freedom, Steve was burdened to reach out to others. Thus, he began a small Bible study in his local church in 1996. This grew and developed and has now reached out to thousands within our local community who have struggled with stubborn habits and addiction.

Since its start, RU has worked to improve the quality of life for communities worldwide by providing an array of services for those suffering from the effects of addictions.

More Addiction Recovery Booklets

Cocaine —$4.00 (TRB-001)

Meth —$4.00 (TRB-003)

Weed —$4.00 (TRB-004)

Cutting —$4.00 (TRB-005)

Pornography —$4.00 (TRB-006)

Uppers —$4.00 (TRB-007)

Tobacco —$4.00 (TRB-008)

Heroin —$4.00 (TRB-012)

Eating —$4.00 (TRB-009)

RX —$4.00 (TRB-011)

Huffing —$4.00 (TRB-014)

Acid —$4.00 (TRB-013)

Gambling —$4.00 (TRB-010)

Alcohol —$4.00 (TRB-002)

Steroids —$4.00 (TRB-015)

order online **www.rurecovery.com**
or call **815-986-0460**

PERSONAL RECOVERY KIT

FOR THE PERSON STRUGGLING ALONE IN THEIR ADDICTION
DISCOVER REAL BIBLICAL FREEDOM

FOR THE FRIEND NOT SURE HOW TO HELP
LEARN HOW TO HELP A FRIEND OR FAMILY MEMBER

FOR THE DISCOURAGED OR DEFEATED CHRISTIAN
BECOME A COMMITTED DISCIPLE OF CHRIST

FOR THE PERSON WITH A DESIRE FOR MORE
GET TO KNOW GOD ON A PERSONAL LEVEL

RURECOVERY.COM/GETPRK

Reformers Unanimous
SCHOOLS *of* DISCIPLESHIP

- 6-8 month Bible-based program
- Addiction treatment for men and women
- Intense discipleship for the newly converted
- A perfect place for the young person (18+) who struggle with relationship issues
- A complete staff of well-trained addiction and discipleship specialists

If you or someone you know needs the kind of help that only a residential program can provide, please contact our offices at 866.REFORMU

Don't hesitate...a life may depend on it.

For more information or to fill out an application, visit **ruhomes.org**

Need Help Now? Call our Addiction Helpline 866-REFORMU (866.733.6768)

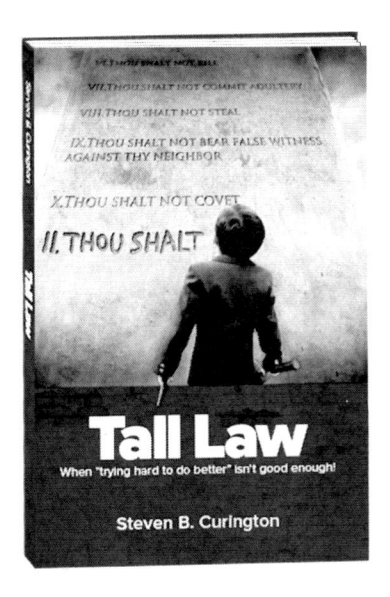

Tall Law
CE-117 $9.95

There are two types of Christian life: the abundant life and the redundant life. One is a life of restful service while the other is a life of discouraging works. How do you attain the real deal? You must understand the foundational truths of biblical behavior modification. If you do not, then you will have to live your life in your power rather than the power of God — and that's a mighty Tall Law! This book is required reading for the Uphold Study Course and can also be used with the student and teacher guide for 26 weeks as Sunday School curriculum.

order online **www.rurecovery.com**
or call **815-986-0460**

Victorious Life Messenger

- Stories of Victory
- The Medical Perspective
- Women of the Word
- Kidz Club
- Full Throttle

Sign Up for the Victorious Life Messenger Blog

The Victorious Life Messenger is a free online blog that includes articles on addiction recovery and testimonies of those who have gained a Victorious Life in Christ, and much more.

Visit **www.rurecovery.com**
or call **815-986-0460**